SUPERSTITIONS ABOUT ANIMALS

FOLKLORE

First Edition 1904
Frank Gibson

New Edition 2019
Edited by Tarl Warwick

COPYRIGHT AND DISCLAIMER

FOREWORD

Treatments of superstition and (technically here applied) cryptozoology can often be fairly boring- enormous volumes full of foot notes; works so numerous that they cannot help but often include one anothers' content. This is thankfully not the case with Gibsons' present work, which refers more to Shakespeare than to biological studies of any rigorous nature.

The content here is rather good and can be parsed roughly into three sub-components; the fantastical, the folkloric, and the more straightly spiritual. The largest proportion is folkloric, dealing with mundane creatures that are said nonetheless to possess characteristics of one non-mundane sort or another; much of the lore is English, some is American, and a bit comes from elsewhere. About half of the same is avian (dealing with birds) which after all is fitting; man spent thousands of years wishing he could fly (amusingly deriding the "silly" ostrich, unable to do so, the whole time- as Gibson himself remarks upon!)

The Bible is often quoted herein as well with regards to the more religious side of animal superstition; the tale of the Donkey and Christ, etc. For the fantastical materials this book speaks at some length about the cockatrice, the basilisk, sea serpents, and more.

This edition of "Superstitions about Animals" has been carefully edited for format and content. Care has been taken to retain all original intent and meaning.

SUPERSTITIONS ABOUT ANIMALS

AUTHOR'S NOTE

My sole object in writing this little book has been to do something towards arousing a more general interest in a subject which has at no time obtained the attention it deserves. Yet there is no subject which so fully repays the thoughtful student as that of Natural History. In bringing together some of the most common superstitions about animals, and dealing with them in a light and popular way, I trust my object will in some measure be attained.

If by the publication of this unpretentious work only a little of the prevalent superstition is swept away, and further interest is created in the wonders of the animal kingdom, I shall be more than amply rewarded.

FRANK GIBSON.
Bishop Auckland,
July 1904.

SUPERSTITIONS ABOUT ANIMALS

INTRODUCTORY

It would be interesting to know at what period of the world's history, and under what circumstances, mankind first attributed to certain members of the animal kingdom powers and functions above and beyond those which they possess through the wisdom of their Creator. Was there, indeed, ever a period when the proper and natural position of each creature was intelligently understood by all mankind, and superstition and credulity were non-existent? If ever there was such a blissful time- and it is reasonable to suppose that in a Divine creation there must have been- how came natural facts of the animal world to be distorted into unreasonable fiction?

How came legends and omens and monstrosities into existence? Did they arise from men's sinfulness and fear, or were they the outcome of fertile imaginations desirous of adding to the wonders of Creation? These are questions that come involuntarily to my mind as I gaze over the great field which my subject embraces, and see the appalling superstition which is rampant in regard to the animal kingdom. For very much of it there is an explanation- men's lamentable ignorance concerning the nature and habits of the various creatures which have been provided for our use and the adornment of the world. But this explanation does not cover the whole range of superstition. It does not provide a solution to the widespread acceptance of omens and signs, or the popular belief in marvelous creatures which have had existence only in unhealthy imagination. The belief in omens and signs is not governed by education or a want of it. A man may have all the education which his age can supply, and his knowledge of natural history may be in keeping with his other mental acquirements, yet he may be as superstitious as the most uncultured and unlearned. In the same way, a man who understands all the good points of a dog, and can explain to you why this part of a certain specimen is too prominent, or why that part ought to be fuller or more angular, may, nevertheless, implicitly believe that the baying of a dog is an infallible sign of an approaching demise. Nor is superstition in respect of the animal kingdom limited to any age or any people. In all ages, so far as we are able to discover, except that which the Creator blessed with His approval, and among 'all tribes and tongues,' superstition has existed in some of its varied forms, and I think I may safely include the present age among the rest. For the amount of ignorance which is still rife in regard to animals; the antiquated ideas which still prevail; the threadbare, ofttimes ludicrous, fables which are still believed in,- do not mark the dawn of the twentieth century as being much more advanced than the first so far as superstitions about animals are concerned. As in the days of Greek and Roman predominance, the raven and the owl, and in a less degree the crow, are still regarded as birds of augury; and while cats in ancient Egypt were exalted to the high estate of deity, the black members of the tribe in our own country are placed above their fellows on account of the good fortune which is said to attend them ; and cats of every color serve as infallible barometers.

If I were to venture outside the limited area of my subject, and the you into the broader field of superstition in general, such as is exemplified by the auguries of crossed knives, thirteen at table, weddings on Fridays, new moons, builders' ladders, and so on, I should have little difficulty in showing that there is much more superstition in our midst than most people would credit. But I must confine myself strictly to the subject embraced by my title, 'Superstitions about Animals.' Within this area I must further limit myself to superstitions which are more or less common to all parts of the country. To go beyond this boundary and deal with superstitions which are purely local, or to include the boundless legends and fables and auguries of other countries, would mean the extension of the work beyond the

SUPERSTITIONS ABOUT ANIMALS

compass of a single volume of more than ordinary dimensions-
indeed, I very much fear the extension would have no ending.

When first I put my pen to paper in the construction
of this little book, I intended to deal with all superstitions so far
as they related to animals, but I quickly perceived where this
intention would lead me. Almost the first omen I took in hand
was that of the Seven Whistlers.

"He the seven birds hath seen, that never part. Seen the
Seven Whistlers in their nightly rounds. And counted them."
-Wordsworth.

But not only did I find that the Seven Whistlers are
regarded as auguries of evil in several parts of the country,
ranging from the north to the south; I also found that omens of a
very similar kind, though under different names, are among the
most popular superstitions. On reading again that delightful work
of Buckland's 'Curiosities of Natural History,' I observed, for
example, that there are certain ill-omened 'whistlers' on the south
coast of England called by the fishermen of Dover the 'Herring
Piece,' and the fishermen of Folkestone the 'Herring Spar.' We
may gather from Spenser's reference to "The whistler shrill that
whoso heares doth dy," that these aerial 'whistlings' are ominous
sounds of considerable antiquity. Almost all local superstitions
may be found under similar manifestations in other parts of the
country, and, in some cases, on the Continent and even wider
afield.

Thus the legend of "Gabriel's hounds Doomed, with
their impious lord, the flying hart To chase for ever, on aerial
grounds," is but another form of several ancient West of England
stories; and of the same order are the Aerial Hunter of
Fontainebleau Forest and The Wild Huntsman of Germany.

SUPERSTITIONS ABOUT ANIMALS

"The Wildgrave flies o'er bush and thorn
With many a shriek of helpless woe;
Behind him hound, and horse, and horn.
And 'Harkaway and holla, ho!'"

Without giving further examples, it will, I think, be seen that had I carried out my first intention of dealing with each local superstition, I should have undertaken a work of far greater magnitude than I anticipated. I therefore decided that I must, at any rate for the present, considerably limit my sphere of operations. I should have liked also to deal with that branch of superstition which, for want of a better term, I may call 'Animal Nostrums'- that is to say, potions and charms made from various parts of animals for the purpose of curing or keeping away maladies; such, for instance, as that mentioned by Pliny- the gall of a hedgehog mixed with the; brains of a bat for removing superfluous hairs; the right eye of a hedgehog fried in oil to render the vision as good at night as in the day; the hair of a mad dog to cure hydrophobia; black cat's hairs for removing stys; adder fat for curing burns or snake bites; viper broth for skin diseases; the ears of a hare to prevent harm or accident- a charm I saw worn by an Irish Yeoman during the Boer War to ward off the enemy's bullets; and so on. But interesting as these nostrums are in exemplifying the extraordinary ignorance and credulity which existed among apothecaries and people in bygone days, and which exist to no small degree among country folk today, I could not do otherwise than leave them till another occasion. For the present, as I have intimated, I will deal only with such superstitions about animals as are more or less known in all parts of the country; and in doing this I will divide my subject into three parts:

1. Signs and omens,
2. Distortion of facts of Natural History.
3. Creatures of the imagination.

SUPERSTITIONS ABOUT ANIMALS

SIGNS AND OMENS

"Stones have been known to move and trees to speak;
Augurs and understood relations have
By magot-pies and choughs and rooks brought forth
The secret'st man of blood."
-Shakespeare.

History tells us that in almost all ages signs and omens have played no small part in affecting men's conduct, and perhaps, in a lesser degree, this is true of the world today. There are, at the present time, a large number of people, by no means ignorant or naturally credulous, who accept omens and signs as the direct manifestations of the Creator's will. They argue that it is compatible with reason that "the birds of the air and beasts of the field" should, under given circumstances, serve a purpose outside their usual and natural spheres. This possibility I will not deny.

If God so will, He can use any part of His marvelous Creation to interpret His purposes, just as He has drawn lessons from the lily and the sparrow. But I must suggest that very few of the various omens, good or ill, are calculated to fill the ordinary mind with a sense of the supernatural. Moreover, the omens are of a too general and unpractical character to be considered seriously. We are told for example, that the baying of a dog is a certain forewarning of death. Now, as a dog rarely confines its vocal exercises to the hearing of any person in particular, the omen is without force. It is quite within the bounds of probability that soon after such an occurrence one of the numerous persons who heard it may die. But what will that prove? If, whenever a dog howled, all the people who heard it died, or if only two persons heard it and one died, leaving the other as a witness, then the reputation of the dog as a kind of agent in advance for a

SUPERSTITIONS ABOUT ANIMALS

future state would be established. Similarly, a 'Death-watch' may be heard by a large number of people among whom there will probably be someone who will subsequently trace the death of a relative to the warning 'tick' of the little beetle.

But let us not be too hasty in poking fun at the superstitions of other people. It is more than likely we have our own pet omens and signs, or believe implicitly in the existence of some strange creatures which have no place in the animal world. Perhaps we do not believe that dogs foretell death, but we are certain that toads are 'venomous'; and though we laugh at the superstition that 'deathwatches' give fatal warning, we are sure that dragons are living realities because they are mentioned in the Bible. All the same, if we are superstitious, we need not fear that we are superstitious in solitude, for many of the ablest and most prominent men in all countries have had their pet omens and signs. Shakespeare, as we shall see, has introduced many superstitions into his writings, and some wonderful creatures of imagination have been allowed to find their way even into the Holy Scriptures.

ILL OMENS

> "Among us mortals, omens drear
> Fright and perplex."
> -Keats.

Let us now notice some of the creatures which are, or have been in earlier days, regarded as ominous of bad fortune. First of all there is the Raven. From the earliest ages the raven has been regarded as one of the 'fatall birds,'

> "Such as by nature men abhorre and hate."

No doubt its solitary habits, its grim plumage, its harsh

voice, and its uncleanliness have been the cause of this general aversion. Noah, we are told, sent out a raven, which went forth to and fro until the waters were dried up. The reason plainly was that there were numerous putrefying carcasses on which it could feed. The dove, which was subsequently sent out, returned to the. Ark because she "found no rest for the sole of her foot."

Probably from that very day the raven has been a pariah among birds, while the dove has always been a type of constancy, love, and gentleness. The raven has become "The fittest bird for murder's track."

The dove is "The very blessed spirit of peace."

But was it not the raven, "Swift-winged and strong,'" which Noah selected, in preference to all other birds, to send forth from the Ark on its lonely voyage of discovery, and was it not the raven which God Himself chose to minister tenderly to the needs of His prophet in the wilderness? As a fact of natural history, devotion and constancy are very strong points in the character of ravens, while bickering and quarrelsomeness run riot in every dove-cote over the most trivial matters. It is in the manner of feeding that the raven appears at its worst, stripping carcasses and devouring the young of other creatures, whereas the dove is very strictly clean in its choice of food. The jet-like blackness of the raven's plumage is another feature which has told strongly against it, while the soft, pale plumage of the dove, contrasted with the sooty garment of the larger bird, is one of the favorite themes of poets- as if, indeed, it were "the coat that made the man." But, as we shall see presently, the raven is not the only bird which has been saddled with a bad character for being black. Then, again, the lonely situation of the raven's place of abode has also been a strong factor in determining its character. Writers have not been slow in laying hold of this habit for the purpose of illustration.

SUPERSTITIONS ABOUT ANIMALS

When Isaiah wished to depict the utter desolation which was to fall upon Idumea he exclaimed: "The owl and the raven shall dwell in it."

The raven is frequently associated with night as typifying evil. Edgar Allan Poe addresses it as coming from "The night's plutonian shore." Aldrich describes night as "a stealthy raven Wrapt to the eyes in his black wings." And, generally speaking, its character is unwholesome and repugnant.

"The eye that mocketh at his father, and despiseth to obey his mother, the ravens of the valley shall pick it out." -Proverbs.

"The croaking raven doth bellow for revenge." -Shakespeare.

"The obscene ravens, clamorous o'er the dead." -Shelley.

"The raven was screeching, the leaves fast fell. The sun gazed cheerlessly down on the sight." -Heine.

These passages serve to show what have been regarded as the habits and nature of the bird. For evidence respecting its character as a bird of ill omen we can go to numerous writers. Edgar Allen Poe, in his magnificent play upon words, 'The Raven,' says:

> "I betook myself to linking
> Fancy into fancy, thinking what this ominous bird of yore,
> What this grim, ungainly, ghastly, gaunt, and ominous bird of yore
> Meant in croaking ' Never more.'"

SUPERSTITIONS ABOUT ANIMALS

Shakespeare more than once mentions the raven as a bird of ill omen. In Macbeth, for example, we find the reference:

"The raven himself is hoarse
That croaks the fatal entrance of Duncan
Under our battlements."

And in Othello we have the lines:

"It comes o'er my memory
As doth the raven o'er the infected house.
Boding to all."

Ben Jonson, in his unfinished play. The Sad Shepherd, writes:

"Now o'erhead sat a raven,
On a sere bough a grown great bird, and hoarse!
Who, all the while the deer was breaking up.
So croaked and cried for it, as all the huntsmen.
Especially old Scathlock, thought it ominous;
Swore it was Mother Maudlin."

Dryden similarly writes:

"Besides, a raven from a withered oak
Left of their lodging was observed to croak.
That omen liked him not."

Even Dr. Watts joins in the general denunciation of the unfortunate fowl:

"Unlucky birds of hateful name-
Ravens and crows."

SUPERSTITIONS ABOUT ANIMALS

And Butler, writing of these two birds in a similar strain, asks "Is it not ominous in all countries. When crows and ravens croak on trees?"

If I were to answer this question, I should be compelled to acknowledge that in all ages, so far as we can ascertain, crows and ravens have indeed been birds of ill omen. Even if we go back to. The century preceding Christ's birth, we find Virgil writing of "The hoarse raven on the blasted bough," which, "By croaking from the left, presaged the coming blow." And this ancient belief in the raven's gift of augury was just as prevalent in the earlier days of Grecian predominance. The ancients attached very grave importance to the auguries of birds, and their note and manner of flight were studiously observed and used in the art of soothsaying. Spenser refers to this art in the words:

> "And tryed time yet taught me greater thinges:
> The soothe of byrdes by beating of their winges."

Mrs. Browning, in Prometheus Bound, also mentions the ancient auguries:

> "And defined as plain
> The wayside omens- flights of crook-clawed birds,
> Showed which are, by their nature, fortunate,
> And which not so."

Jonson, at some length, in The Masque of Augurs, deals with this special branch of 'the tuneful art of augury';

> "*Apollo* (singing). Then forth and show the several flights
> Your birds have made, or what the wing
> Or voice in augury doth bring,
> Which hand the crow cried on, how high

SUPERSTITIONS ABOUT ANIMALS

The vulture or the heme did fly;
What wing the swan made, and the dove,
The stork, and which did get above;
Show all the birds of food or prey,
The night-crow, swallow, or the kite,
Let these have neither right.
   Chorus. Nor part.
   In this night's art.
Apollo: (after the auguries are interpreted). The signs are
lucky all, and right.
There hath not been a voice, or flight,
Of ill presage
Linus: The bird that brings
Her augury alone to kings,
The dove, hath flown.-
Orpheus: And to thy (King James I.) peace,
Fortune and the Fates increase.
Branchus: Minerva's hernshaw, and her owl,
Do both proclaim, thou shalt control
The course of things.
Idmon: As now they be
With tumult carried,
Apollo: And live free
From hatred, faction, or the fear
To blast the olive thou dost wear."

I need hardly say that in those ancient days of prevalent
credulity the raven, the owl, and the crow were made the
subjects of many weird legends. None of these, I think, is
quainter than how the raven, or as another rendering has it, the
crow, was transformed from swan-like whiteness to the very
extreme, the most funereal black. It was on account of his
'chattering tongue,' or his desire to be the first bringer of evil
news, as Ovid informs us, that the raven lost his pristine beauty,
and was allowed no longer to perch among white birds, "This

bird was formerly of a silver hue," says the ancient writer (translated by Henry T. Riley, M.A.), "with snow-white feathers, so that he equaled the doves, entirely without spot; nor would he give place to the geese that were to save the Capitol by their watchful voice, nor to the swan haunting the streams. His tongue was the cause of his disgrace; his chattering tongue being the cause, that the color which was white is passage in now the reverse." Or as Addison renders the same passage in verse:

> "The raven once in snowy plumes was drest,
> White as the whitest dove's unsullied breast,
> Fair as the guardian of the Capitol,
> Soft as the swan, a large and lovely fowl;
> His tongue, his prating tongue had changed him quite
> To sooty blackness from the purest white."

The raven, bird of Phoebus, having discovered that Larisssen Coronis, than whom "there was no one more beauteous in all Haemonia," had been unfaithful to his master, winged his way to the god and informed him of his mistress's infidelity.

"On hearing the crime of his mistress his laurel fell down; and at the same moment his usual looks, his plectrum, and his color, forsook the god. And as his mind was now burning with swelling rage, he took up his wonted arms, and leveled his bow bent from the extremities, and pierced with an unerring shaft, that bosom that had been so often pressed to his own breast. Wounded, she uttered a groan, and, drawing the steel from out of the wound, she bathed her white limbs with purple blood; and... poured forth her life together with her blood. A deadly coldness took possession of her body deprived of life. The lover, too late, alas! repents of his cruel vengeance, and blames himself that he listened to the bird, and that he was so infuriated. He hates the bird, through which he was forced to know of the crime, and the cause of his sorrow; he hates, too, the string, the bow, and his hand; and together with his hand, those rash weapons, the arrows. He cherishes her fallen to the ground, and by late resources endeavors to conquer her destiny; and in vain he practices his physical arts... And he forbade the raven, expecting for himself the reward of his tongue that told no untruth, to perch any longer among the white birds."

So that is how the raven became black! But the awe and reverence with which the ancients regarded it in time changed to loathing and detestation. Its mission, as a prophet by which evil things might be averted, no longer obtained, and it became simply an 'unclean fowl' whose associations were loathsome and deadly.

"While o'er those caitiffs where they lie.
The wolf shall snarl, the ravens cry."

Even in resting, it evinced a preference for decay:

"O'erhead sat a raven
On a sere bough." -Jonson

"Or raven on a blasted oak." -Scott.

"e passes now the doddered oak.
Ye heard the startled raven croak" -Scott.

"A raven from a withered oak." -Dryden.

As the ensign of the devastating Danes, it struck terror into the bold hearts of our forefathers,

"When Denmark's raven soared on high.
Triumphant through Northumbrian sky.
Till hovering near, her fatal croak

SUPERSTITIONS ABOUT ANIMALS

Bade Reged's Britons dread the yoke,
And the broad shadow of her wing
Blackened each cataract and spring.
-Scott.

Its very eyes have been likened to living coals or flashes of fire.

"Thus I sat engaged in guessing, but no syllable expressing To the fowl whose fiery eyes now burned into my bosom's core."
-E. A. Foe.

"And aloft upon the ridge-pole
Kahgahgee, the King of Ravens,
Sat with fiery eyes."
-Longfellow.

"Why, any time of night, you may see his eyes in my dark room, shining like two sparks. And every night, and all night too, he's broad awake."
-Dickens.

In addition to being universally regarded as uncanny, and mostly branded as a 'thing of evil,' the raven has not escaped being directly associated with the Realms of Darkness. Edgar Allan Poe had no doubt that its origin was distinctly 'evil,' and it would seem that his secret opinion of the immortal 'Raven' was that it also consisted both of 'fiend' and 'devil.'

But Charles Dickens is in no way dubious respecting the origin of the equally immortal 'Grip.' He tells us that the bird "asserted his brimstone birth and parentage with great distinctness," and Grip, "as if exulting in his infernal character," persistently declared, whenever he had the opportunity, "I'm a devil, I'm a devil!"

There is, perhaps, scarcely need to say that the character of the raven has been stigmatized without the least justification. Apart from its universal association with evil augury, it has always been regarded as a cruel parent, turning its young out of their nest before they have learned to provide for their own sustenance; whereas, no bird existing is more solicitous concerning the welfare of its young than is the raven. As we have seen from two of the foregoing quotations, the Crow is mentioned in company with the raven as 'a thing of evil,' and its character as a bird of 'ill omen' seems to be equally ancient.

No doubt its color, which has made its name proverbial, together with its nasty habits, have singled it out for popular disfavor. Like the raven, it is generally associated with death and decay, and its chosen resting-place is away from color and foliage.

"A crow with sidelong eye
Watched from a dead bough."

In another respect also it resembles its larger relative the raven- its plumage was formerly white, at any rate so we are told, and its transformation was in the same way brought about by the unguarded use of a chattering tongue. The story is in all respects like that of Phoebus and Coronis, but is well worth repeating in the quaint, homely language of the poet Chaucer. Says he:

"When Phebus dwelled here in erth adoun,
As olde bookes maken mentioun,
He was the most lusty bacheler
Of all this world, and eke the best archer."

SUPERSTITIONS ABOUT ANIMALS

And taking him all round he was

"The semelieste man
That is or was, sithen the world began."

"Now had this Phebus in his house a crowe.
Which in a cage he fostered many a day.
And taught it speken, as men teche a jay.
Whit was this crowe, as is a snow-whit swan,
And contrefete the speche of every man
He coude, when he shulde tell a tale.
Therwith in all this world no nightingale
He coude by an hundred thousand del
Singen so wonder merily and wel."

But Phebus possessed more than a crow in a cage:

"Now had this Phebus in his hous a wif,
Which that he loved more than his lif,
And night and day did ever his diligence
Hire for to plese, and don hire reverence."

Phebus, however, was a jealous man, and tried to keep
his 'wife' from receiving the attentions of any other swain; but,
says Chaucer, it is 'labour in vain' to watch 'a shrewe,' for they
cannot be watched. Take any bird and put it in a cage, he says,
foster it tenderly with meat and drink, and keep it clean, and,
although the cage be golden, it will 'twenty thousand fold' live in
a forest that is 'wilde and cold' eating worms and 'swiche
wretchednesse.' So also a cat, though fostered and fed on milk
and tender flesh, will leave these dainties if she "see a mous go
by the wall." And so it was with this "Wif Which that he loved
more than his lif."

No sooner was Phebus's back turned than she 'sent for

hire lemman'- sent for her lover- and the crow looked down from his perch, but "sayde never a word."

However, when Phebus returned, the crow opened his heart and his beak and told him how false was this woman whom he loved so truly; and Phebus, thinking his heart was breaking, drew his bow and sent an arrow quivering into his wife's body. Then, filled with remorse for what he had done, he turned Upon the crow furiously and cursed it for making so free use of its scurrilous tongue.

> "And to the crowe, O false thefe, said he,
> I wol thee quite anon thy false tale.
> Thou song whilom, like any nightingale,
> Now Shalt thou, false thefe, thy song forgon,
> And eke thy white feathers, everich on,
> Ne never in all thy lif ne shalt thou speke;
> Thus shul men on a traitour ben awreke.
> Thou and thin ofspring ever shul be blake,
> Ne never swete noise shul ye make.
> But ever crie ageins tempest and rain.
> In token that thrugh thee my wif is slain.
> And to the crowe be stert, and that anon,
> And pulled his white fethers everich on.
> And made him blak, and raft him all his song
> And eke his speche, and out at dore him flong
> Unto the devil, which I him betake;
> And for this cause ben alle crowes blake."

And, pointing a sound moral from the lot of the unfortunate 'crowe,' deprived of its sweet song and snowy plumage, Chaucer sagely adds: "My son, beware, and be non auctour newe (no bearer) Of tidings, whether they ben false or trewe; Wher so thou come, amonges high or lowe, Kepe well thy tonge, and thinke upon the crowe."

SUPERSTITIONS ABOUT ANIMALS

Under certain circumstances the Rook is also regarded as a bird of ill omen. Country people tell us that when a colony of rooks forsake their accustomed building-place it may be accepted as a sure sign that a great calamity is about to fall on the family to whom the rookery belongs; and a single rook sitting lonely upon a house-top is accepted by many as ominous of death. Besides being regarded as birds of ill omen, rooks are supposed to possess the villainous habit of plucking out the eyes of persons sleeping in open places; and it is further said of them that whenever they pass over a corpse they utter a weird, uncanny cry. In respect of the former, it need only be said that rooks are not carnivorous birds like crows or ravens; and as for the latter, I have not yet met with any one who has taken special notice of the birds during a funeral procession, or at an interment, to be able to say how they conduct themselves under such circumstances.

As I have already pointed out, both the crow and the raven have most probably derived much of their unpleasant notoriety from their somber plumage, and it is just as likely that the rook comes under the same category for the same reason. Even our gay, chattering friend, the Jackdaw, is not allowed to go unscathed. Cowper describes it as a bird which

> "By his coat
> And by the hoarseness of his note.
> Might be supposed to be a crow."

And he classes him among "Birds obscene of ominous note," a category in which he also places the Chough, called by some the 'red-billed jackdaw.' Dryden also associates birds of a black feather in one group:

> "To Crows the like impartial grace affords,
> And Choughs and Daws and such republic birds."

SUPERSTITIONS ABOUT ANIMALS

Longfellow includes the Jay among the 'black marauders':

> "Kahgahgee, the king of ravens,
> Gathered all his black marauders,
> Crows and blackbirds, jays and ravens
> Clamorous on the dusky tree-tops."

And, as if there were something threatening in the voices of the 'black marauders,' as 'from all the neighboring tree-tops' they 'cawed and croaked,'

> "'Ugh!' the old men all responded,
> From their seats beneath the pine-trees!"

Shakespeare, as we have seen, gives the Raven a primary place among birds of evil augury, and, in at least one passage, puts the Crow in a similarly notorious position:

> "And thou treble-dated crow,
> That thy sable gender makest
> With the breath thou givest and takest
> 'Mongst our mourners shalt thou go."

Then, as if to complete the list, he adds the Magpie:

> "Augurs and understood relations have
> By magot-pies and choughs and rooks brought forth
> The secret'st man of blood."

It is, however, only when it appears singly that the magpie is a sprognosticator of evil. On the other hand, two or more are said to be indicative of good fortune. Cowper, for instance, asserts that he 'rejoiced' "If two auspicious magpies crossed my way," a reference, evidently, to the old rhyme:

SUPERSTITIONS ABOUT ANIMALS

"One for sorrow,
Two for mirth,
Three for a wedding,
Four for a birth."

The Owl, which not infrequently we find mentioned in company with the raven, bears the same character as a foreteller of evil. The reason for this may be found in its love of solitude, its habit of turning night into day, its silent, spectral flight, and its melancholy cry. Those who have heard these weird, mournful notes in the dead of night will quite appreciate the prophet Micah's simile when he speaks of the 'Mourning as the owls.'

In South Africa I have heard this 'mourning' or 'hooting' on the kopjes at night, and it is a strange, uncanny cry, quite calculated to create a 'creepy' sensation, if not actually of foreboding. Whenever it is mentioned in Scripture or in poetry, the owl, inclusive of all the species, is surrounded with an atmosphere of gloom, sadness, and solitude. The Psalmist leads the way in this respect by writing of 'the owl of ruined places.' Isaiah, when he describes the downfall of Idumea, says: "The screech owl (or night-monster) shall rest there. There shall the great owl rest, and gather under her shadow."

Gray, in his immortal "Elegy," describes this feature in the following beautiful lines:

"Save that from yonder ivy-mantled tower,
The moping owl doth to the moon complain
Of such as, wand'ring near her secret bow'r,
Molest her ancient, solitary reign."

In the same strain Burns, in his charmingly expressed ode 'To the Owl,' writes:

SUPERSTITIONS ABOUT ANIMALS

"Shut out, lone bird! from all the feather'd train.
To tell thy sorrows to th' unheeding gloom:
No friend to pity when thou dost complain,
Grief all thy thought, and solitude thy home."

Truly a beautifully-worded but melancholy, and, in one sense, an inaccurate description. There is no adequate reason to suppose that the owl is a more unhappy bird than, say, the canary or the skylark. No doubt it is solely the nocturnal habits of the 'lone bird' which have surrounded it with an atmosphere so gloomy and pathetic. The song of the nightingale, probably for the same reason, has in it a vein of sweet melancholy which is not to be found ill the song of the robin, or the lark, or any other day-time warbler.

In nearly all references to the owl as a bird of evil omen, the species mentioned is the screech owl, or, as we know it in England, the 'barn owl.':

"But thou shrieking harbinger,
Foul precursor of the fiend.
Augur of the fever's end,
To this troop come thou not near!"
-Shakespeare.

As far back as history takes us, and in all countries where the unfortunate bird is known, it has been burdened with the foulest character of any of the 'feathered tribe.' To go back only to the days of Rome, Virgil writes:

"With a boding note
The solitary screech owl strains his throat.
And on a chimney-top, or turret height.
With song obscene disturbs the silence of the night."

SUPERSTITIONS ABOUT ANIMALS

And, speaking of the same period, Butler writes:

"The Roman senate, when within
The city wall an owl was seen,
Did cause their clergy with lustrations
The round-faced prodigy t' avert
From doing town or country hurt."

Ovid, writing in the same strain, speaks of the owl as 'an accursed bird,' and further describes Aescalaphus as becoming "An obscene bird, the foreboder of approaching woe, a lazy owl, a direful omen to mortals." Hardly is it necessary to say that among the ancients the screech owl was the subject of numerous legends, each of which emphasizes its character as a bird of ill repute. Nothing shows more clearly how cordially was this bird detested, though at the same time feared, than the fable of Nyctimene's transformation into an owl for committing a heinous crime.

And it is because of this foul sin, so the ancient legend says, that the owl secludes herself from the company of all other birds and ventures forth only under cover of darkness. "She is a bird indeed; but being conscious of her crime she avoids the human gaze and the light, and conceals her shame in the darkness; and by all the birds she is expelled entirely from the sky." -Ovid.

Coming to medieval days, we find that the character of the owl has not improved in popular opinion.

"The ghastlie owl her grievous inne (abode) doth keep." -Spenser.

While Shakespeare, writing about the same period, makes several references to the bird's illboding tongue, among

SUPERSTITIONS ABOUT ANIMALS

which are the following:

"Whilst the screech owl, screeching loud,
Puts the wretch that lies in woe,
In remembrance of a shroud."
-A Midsummer Nights Dream.

"Bring forth that fatal screech owl to our house,
That nothing sung but death to us and ours;
Now death shall stop his dismal threatening sound,
And his ill-boding tongue no more shall speak."
-Henry VIII (Part III.).

Still in later days the owl retains its notoriety;

"Again the shriek-owl shrieks- ungracious sound !
I'll hear no more; it makes one's blood run cold."
-Robert Blair.

"What yonder rings .' what yonder sings?
Why shrieks the owlet grey?...
'Tis death-bells' clang, 'tis funeral song.
The body to the clay" -Scott.

"The bird of omen with incessant scream,
To melancholy thoughts awakes the soul."
-Chatterton.

"A monstrous owl across us flies.
Bad omen- this new match can't be a happy one."
-Keats.

"Down in a dark and solitary vale.
Where the screech owl sings her fatal tale."
-Chatterton.

SUPERSTITIONS ABOUT ANIMALS

"No Fatal Owle the Bedstead keeps.
With direful notes to fright your sleeps."
-Herrick,

Ben Jonson writes of the "shrieks of luckless owls"; Keats, the "gloom-bird's hated screech"; Cowper, "the boding owl"; Moore, "the deathbird's cry"; Byron, "the owlet whose notes the dark fiend of midnight deplores." And many another poet joins these in denouncing the unlucky fowl as "a thing of evil." To reset an old-time adage- "Give an owl a bad name and shoot it." And this is precisely what happens to the poor bird.

What with collectors and gamekeepers and sportsmen, the owl's life usually is short and none too sweet. In the destruction of these useful birds gamekeepers are the greatest offenders. "Kill everything but game " seems to be the rule by which these men are guided, so they shoot all manner of 'vermin' from owls to jays and woodpeckers. To make a careful and intelligent study of the woodland Inhabitants which they see from day to day does not seem to them to be a course they should pursue. If they studied the nature and habits of owls they would not be long in discovering that the 'bird of ill omen' was their friend and not their enemy. Because now and again an owl has been seen with a young pheasant in its possession, seems conclusive enough evidence to the ordinary keeper that it is a marauder which must forthwith be put out of the way of doing further harm.

But it is a rare occurrence for an owl to seek young pheasants for food; and when it has been discovered with this kind of game in its possession, the young pheasant would, I think, on examination prove to be a delicate straggler. Even supposing that an owl actually does now and again pick up a small bird, can this be fairly set against the vast number of rats and mice which it kills as its natural food? Of very different

SUPERSTITIONS ABOUT ANIMALS

habits and appearance from the owl is the graceful Lapwing, wheeling and 'lapping' in its lazy flight. Who would suppose that so pretty and harmless a bird as this tufted frequenter of our meadows would commend itself to the imagination of superstitious minds? Yet the lapwing has long been regarded in Scotland as a bird of ill omen. Grahame, in his Birds of Scotland, more than once refers to the lapwing as an augury of evil, and gives the story from which it derived its evil character. So the story goes, when the sturdy Covenanters were seeking refuge among the wilds of Scotland from the persecution of the King's troops, the lapwings, hovering over the heads of the refugees, betrayed their whereabouts to the keen eyes of their pursuers. And so it came to pass that the lapwing has become known in Scotland as a bird of 'ill omen.' Poor, unfortunate waller! How much of the story is fact, and how much is of the same loose imagination that has made the yellowhammer a pariah among birds, and the wren a malignant atom to be ruthlessly hunted down on St. Stephen's Day? But perhaps we can go back centuries before the days of the Covenanters for the origin of the lapwing's ill repute, for was it not into the likeness of one of these graceful birds that cruel King Tereus was transformed when pursuing with his drawn sword the outraged Philomela? As Spenser puts it:

> "The Thracian king lamenting sore,
> Turned to a lapwing, doeth them uprayde;"

...and Chaucer, no doubt thinking of the same fable; "The false lapwing, full of trecherie." Or, as a Milanese song renders the ancient legend:

> "There once was a king
> As wicked as possible;
> The Lord changed him
> Into a upoe."

SUPERSTITIONS ABOUT ANIMALS

But in England the ancient myth is associated with the lapwing and not the hoopoe, though each is a bird "upon whose head stands a crested plume." This promiscuous interchanging of the names may be found in the lists of unclean fowl mentioned in Leviticus and Deuteronomy, where the same bird is rendered by the Authorized Version 'lapwing,' and by the Revised Version 'hoopoe,' the latter rendering also being supported by the Vulgate. Or it may be that the lapwing's unpleasant notoriety is derived solely from its melancholy cry, in the same way that the owl unquestionably is hated for its 'dismal, threatening sound,' its 'fatal screech.' In any case, the two great poets of Scotland, who must have been often within hearing of its wailful voice, and have noted its weird, circling flight, have given it an atmosphere of gloom and melancholy. Burns, when solicitous for the peace of his Mary sleeping by 'Sweet Afton,' admonishes the bird in the lines:

> "Thou green-crested lapwing, thy screaming forbear,
> I charge you disturb not my slumbering fair."

And Sir Walter Scott, writing of the 'gentle lover of nature' who was found dead on Helvellyn, says:

> "And more stately thy couch by this desert lake lying.
> Thy obsequies sung by the grey plover flying."

So that, when we are walking in the stillness of the evening, and we hear near at hand a sad, wailful scream like some 'lost soul forlorn,' we may remember that we are listening to the 'foreboding' cry which brought destruction to the sturdy bands of Covenanters, and sang the obsequies over the stark body of the poor dead 'lover of nature!' Or, if our fancy turns to higher flights, we can, in the same stillness, think that here the lustful King of Thrace, turned into a lapwing, for ever wails the ravishment of poor, confiding Philomela. Another bird which is regarded as a bird of ill omen is the Stormy Petrel. Sailors firmly believe that the petrel is a precursor of stormy weather. Theodore Watt mentions this strange belief when he writes: "Bird whom I welcomed, while the sailors -cursed."

And Procter, writing in the same strain, declares that:

"The petrel telleth her tale in vain,
For the mariner curseth the warning bird
Which bringeth him news of the storm unheard."

It would scarcely be supposed that among the creatures which are said to foretell a calamity, superstitious people have included the common domestic Pigeon. There is nothing in the appearance or habits of this pretty, stately bird which should place it on the black list of birds of ill omen, and certainly under ordinary conditions its name is not associated with anything that is evil; but there is one aspect under which it is regarded by many people to be a sure foreteller of death- that is when it enters a room through an open window. Now, personally I regard with something like ridicule so simple a form of superstition, and would give a welcome to any strange pigeon which did me the honor of seeking a refuge in my room. But, notwithstanding, I can recall the actual case of an old friend of mine dying in a room where a pigeon had a few days previously entered by the window. The pigeon happened to be one of my own, and my aged friend lectured me pretty severely on allowing the bird to spoil the neatness of his apartment. He was hale and hearty at the time, but a few days later he died in that very room. Not long ago I mentioned this incident casually to a friend, and although he had not heard of the superstition associated with it, he curiously enough declared that a week before the death of his mother a stray pigeon was caught in the room in which she subsequently died.

SUPERSTITIONS ABOUT ANIMALS

These two remarkable incidents, quoted from my own experience, will no doubt be considered conclusive evidence, by some of my readers, that under the circumstances stated a pigeon is a sure foreteller of death; but we must not so quickly jump to illogical conclusions. A starling- much more somber and harsh-voiced than any pigeon- which recently I captured in a neighbor's room, might just as reasonably be accepted as a fore-warner of death. Whereas it is more sensible to suppose that the affrighted bird which so energetically nibbled at my thumbs, accidentally fluttered down the chimney and heartily wished himself back on the chimney-top instead of in a strange room, poked and peered at by his mortal enemy man.

Similar to the above-mentioned superstitions is the belief that a swallow alighting on a windowsill foretells death to some person residing in, or associated with persons living in, the house. But a falling picture also, we are told, forewarns us of the same calamity, and there are many other incidents equally portentous which I need not mention. One, however, is worth dealing with somewhat fully, as it is almost universally accepted as a sign of approaching death. The fateful augur, in this case, is the little beetle (Anobium striatum), or, as it is commonly known, the 'Death watch,' which, by its quaint 'ticking' or tapping, sets people's hearts a-beating apprehensively. Who has not, at one time or another, heard this little creature playing his merry pranks in the wainscotting or cupboard when everything else has been silent?

Not very long ago I heard one of these 'death watches' which, I was told, had been 'ticking' at intervals for several weeks, but no one in the farmhouse where it was located has died in consequence. As a matter of fact, one of the occupants of the room soon afterwards married very happily, and the other is now holding a responsible position in South Africa. So much for the fateful ticking of this particular specimen! In reality, putting

SUPERSTITIONS ABOUT ANIMALS

all superstition aside, the frail little creature, which so innocently has earned an unenviable character, 'ticks' for no other purpose than to attract the attention of its mate. Under like circumstances the coster, who whistles under his donah's window when he wishes her to come out for a stroll, should be regarded by the superstitious as a creature of ill omen.

Several of our poets have assisted in keeping alive this old-time superstition. Dean Swift mentions it in the following lines, though in a desire to particularize he erroneously describes the 'death watch' as 'a worm' or 'a maggot':

"A wood worm,
That lies in old wood like a hare in her form,
With teeth or with claws it will bite or will scratch,
And chambermaids christen this worm ' death watch';
Because like a watch it always cries ' click.'
For sure as a gun they will give up the ghost
If the maggot cries 'click' when it scratches the post."

Gay also refers to the 'death watch' in the passage;

"The wether's bell
Before the drooping flock toll'd forth her knell,
The solemn death -watch clicked the hour she died."

Similarly, Wordsworth adjures us to:

"Take
A fearful apprehension from the owl
Or death watch"

Walter Thornbury, in his dramatic description of 'The Death of th' Owd Squire,' tells us that "The death watch, sure enough, tick'd loud just over th'owd mare's head, Tho' he'd never

SUPERSTITIONS ABOUT ANIMALS

once been heard up there since master's boy lay dead."

And Tennyson, in his poem " Forlorn," gives the old superstition in the words:

> "You that lie with wasted lungs
> Waiting for your summons...
> In the night, O the night!
> O the death watch beating"

The Baying of a Dog as a sure foretelling of death is one of the most ancient and widespread superstitions. Certainly nothing can so easily create a feeling of awe and apprehension as the weird, uncanny howling of a dog in the dead of night. Any one may justly be excused a superstitious belief in this respect. Never shall I forget the hideous howling of a retriever at midnight some years ago, when I was sailing in the Black Sea- or, to be more accurate, perhaps I ought to use the more applicable word 'baying,' for the noise, as distinguishable from mere howling, was like a hopeless wail. The night was as dark as pitch; that awful darkness which is peculiar to the sea. There was no sound save the panting of the engines and the beating of the propeller. I was sitting in my cabin reading for a brief spell before turning in, when of a sudden there arose, close to my door, such a villainous,, unearthly baying that my blood seemed to turn cold in my veins, and I believe my hair stood upright.

More than anything, it might have been the cry of a soul shut out from Everlasting Life. Then everything was still again. A moment later the negro steward rushed into the cabin, with his big eyes rolling and his black face twitching with abject fright. "One of us has got to die, sir," he cried. "The dog howl, and it means death. One of us bound to die."

It seems almost as good as verifying the superstition to

say that, within a few days, a sailor was killed on the very spot
where the retriever had howled. Such, however, is a fact, and I
had the unhappy duty of holding the poor fellow in my arms
when, in great agony, he drew his last breath. Many allusions are
made in our own literature to this superstition. In Shakespeare's
King Henry VI. we have a direct reference to the howling of
dogs as 'an evil sign,' and among others of his plays there are
also passages in which the howling is attended with most dismal
phenomena. The reference mentioned is:

> "The owl shrieked at thy birth, an evil sign,
> The night-crow cried, aboding trickless time,
> Dogs howled, and hideous tempests tore down trees."

In 'Cumnor Hall,' a poem by W. J. Mickle, which
suggested to Sir Walter Scott the groundwork of his romance
Kenilworth, there is a reference to the superstition:

> "The death-bell thrice was heard to ring,
> An aerial voice was heard to call.
> And thrice the raven flapped his wing
> Around the towers of Cumnor Hall.
> The mastiff howled at village door.
> The oaks were shattered on the green;
> Woe was the hour, for never more
> That hapless Countess e'er was seen."

It may be merely a coincidence, but there are three
incidents common to the two foregoing quotations. When
Gloucester was born, so Shakespeare makes King Henry say, the
night-crow cried, dogs howled, and trees were torn down. At the
death of the Countess, Mickle tells us, an aerial voice called, the
mastiff howled, and oaks were shattered; and if we extend the
passage in King Henry VI, we find that there is yet another
common feature: "The raven rook'd her on the chimney's top;"

or, as 'Cumnor Hall' has it: "Thrice the raven flapped his wing."

Among Keats's poems we also find the superstition directly referred to: "For as among mortals omens drear fright and perplex, Dog's howl or gloom-birds hated screech."

In the quotations from Shakespeare and Keats we find that the howling is accepted as an omen of evil things not come to pass; whereas, in 'Cumnor Hall,' the howling takes place at the time of the violent death of the Countess. Shakespeare evidently goes beyond the generally accepted significance of the incident in making the animal apprehend, at the birth of Gloucester, a calamity which was not to take place until he had reached manhood. But in the other quotations we have direct references to what is a common belief, far more common than many will credit, that dogs, with a finer sense than human beings possess, are able to see spirits.

In this country the supposition is that dogs see the spirits of those who, loosed from mortal flesh, move about in the world of space which envelops our Earth; or that, by even a finer sense, like that attributed to the shark, they are able to foreknow of death's approach or discern its presence. Shakespeare, no doubt familiar with this belief, associates the howling of the ban dogs with the midnight hour when spirits are said to be set at liberty, a subject I shall refer to later.

"Ban dogs howl
And spirits walk and ghosts break up their graves."

In the East the popular belief is similar, yet varies in one particular. While in England it is supposed that dogs see ghosts 'in general,' the Eastern belief is that dogs are able to perceive the dread form of the Angel of Death. Sir Richard Burton, the famous traveler, on this point says: "There are also certain

SUPERSTITIONS ABOUT ANIMALS

superstitions about the dog resembling ours, only, as usual more poetical and less grotesque, current in El Hejaz. Most people believe that when the animal howls without apparent cause in the neighborhood of a house, it forebodes death to one of the inmates. For the dog, they say, can distinguish the awful form of Azrael, the angel of death, hovering over the doomed abode, whereas man's spiritual sight is dull and dim by reason of his sins."

In Longfellow's 'Golden Legend' there is a conversation between a Jewish Rabbi and Judas Iscariot touching upon the same superstition:

"Rabbi. Come hither, Judas Iscariot.
Say, if thy lesson thou hast got
From thy Rabbinical Book or not.
Why howls the dog at night?
Judas. In the Rabbinical Book, it saith
The dogs howl, when, with icy breath
Great Sammael, the Angel of Death,
Takes through the town his flight!"

Among sailors there is a very common superstition, that a Shark following in the wake of a vessel unmistakably foretells the death of some person on board. Such a belief is, so far as I personally have had the opportunity of observing, without the least foundation in fact. On a voyage to South Africa a few years ago I noticed, when nearing the Equator, that a very large, sinister-looking shark kept up with the vessel for many miles, but the passage concluded under the most favorable and happy circumstances; no one died, and very few were even sea-sick. Curiously enough, however, when I returned to England on a large liner fitted up as a hospital ship, with accommodation for more than a thousand invalids, we never sighted a shark from Capetown to Southampton, though there were many cases of

SUPERSTITIONS ABOUT ANIMALS

sickness on board, mid one of the passengers was buried at sea. Probably all the sharks were busy following in the wake of other vessels!

This old superstition is well brought out in a poem entitled 'The Return of the Admiral,' by Procter:

> "How gallantly, how merrily
> We ride along the sea!
> The morning is all sunshine,
> The wind is blowing free:
> The billows are all sparkling,
> And bounding in the light."

But:

> "In our wake, like any servant,
> Follows ever the bold shark."

Then the admiral of the fleet, who:

> "Grew paler
> And paler as we flew,"

> "Spied the creature
> That kept following in our lee."

He seemed to be aware of the direful augury, for:

> "He shook- 'twas but an instant;
> For speedily the pride
> Ran crimson to his heart.
> Till all chances he defied."

But the admiral's defiance was in vain, for:

SUPERSTITIONS ABOUT ANIMALS

That night a horrid whisper
Fell on us where we lay;
And we knew our fine old admiral
Was changing into clay;
And we heard the wash of waters,
Though nothing could we see.
And a whistle and a plunge
Among the billows in our lee!
'Till dawn we watched the body,
In its dead and ghastly sleep;
And next evening, at sunset,
It was slung into the deep!
And never from that moment-
Save one shudder through the sea-
Saw we or heard the shark
That had followed in our lee!"

Of a less dramatic character, but bearing out the old superstition among sailors, is a passage in the biography of the late Rev. Bryan Roe, the well known Wesleyan missionary, who died on the West Coast of Africa:

"Two or three sharks it may be are following in the vessel's wake, attracted, it would seem, by the fact that there is a sick man lying on board, for the old and weather-beaten quartermaster confidentially informs the clerical passenger (Mr. Roe) that he will soon have a burial job on hand. The quartermaster is always an authority on the subject of sharks. 'Them there sharks,' he explains, 'have more sense in them than most Christshuns. They know wot's wot, I can tell yer; doctors ain't in it with sharks. I've heard sharks larf when the doctor has told a sick man he was convalescent- larf, sir, outright, 'cos they knew what a blessed mistake he was making. They are following up the scent of a man on board now that's going to die, and they'll not leave us until such times be as they gets him.'"

SUPERSTITIONS ABOUT ANIMALS

I am afraid that the "old and weather-beaten quartermaster " was imposing on the credulity of the passengers when he went so far in his sailor-like love of 'yarning' as to picture sharks laughing outright with sinister irony; but his narrative in the main, as it is reported by the biographer, gives a very fair description of the popular superstition among sea-going men. As a matter of fact, I think we may more reasonably assume that sharks follow in the wake of vessels for the same reason that all large fish do, solely for the scraps of meat and other leavings which are thrown overboard. Very probably instances are on record when sharks have been observed following vessels on which a sailor or passenger has subsequently died; but such a coincidence in no way proves that they have scented death, or seen the 'dread form of the Angel of Death.' Why is not the same faculty extended to the porpoises which play around the vessel's bows, or to the 'wailing sea-birds' which hover about the vessel's rigging?

GOOD OMENS

"The signs are lucky all, and right.
There hath not been a voice, or flight,
Of ill presage.
-Ben Jonson.

Happily every creature is not placed on the black list of those whose melancholy mission is to foretell calamities. There are, on the other hand, many whose purpose is said to be exactly the reverse- to augur good luck, peace, happiness; and curiously enough most of these prognosticators are birds.

The Stork, that 'emblem of true piety,' is a bird whose presence is regarded as an augury of good fortune in almost all countries where it is known. In Holland and Germany at the present day the inhabitants give the birds every encouragement

SUPERSTITIONS ABOUT ANIMALS

to make their nests on the roofs of the houses, and fortunate is the man supposed to be whose house the storks choose for this purpose. Longfellow, in an American song, 'To the Stork,' very beautifully illustrates this belief:

"Welcome, O Stork! that dost wing
Thy flight from far away!
Thou hast brought us the signs of spring,
Thou hast made our sad hearts gay.
Descend, O Stork! descend
Upon our roof to rest;
In our ash-tree, O my friend.
My darling, make thy nest."

In the 'Golden Legend' the same poet represents the bird as a direct gift from God. Speaking of the good Prince Henry, Bertha asks:

"Did he give us the beautiful stork above
On the chimney-top, with its large round nest?"

And Gottlicb replies:

"No, not the stork. By God in heaven,
As a blessing, the dear white stork was given."

The reverence for the stork dates back to very ancient times. The Egyptians paid it the Same reverence as the sacred Ibis; the Thessalonians were restricted from doing the bird an injury; the Romans regarded it as a bird of good augury. A Greek law compelling children to maintain their aged parents took its name from the bird, and all the numerous legends which have been woven round its name testify to its devotion, faithfulness, love, and, generally speaking, its sterling character. Was it not into a stork that the pitying gods transformed Antigone when, boastful of her beautiful hair, the jealous Juno turned her locks into writhing serpents?

As an example of the stork's devotion to its young ones, we are told that on a fire occurring in the city of Delft, the parent, after making strenuous efforts to rescue them without success, permitted herself to perish with them in the flames. The stork's faithfulness to its mate is brought out in a story that the male bird, rather than desert his partner when she was wounded at the time of migrating, spent the winter months by her side tenderly providing for her needs. Its filial devotion is said to be so great that when the parent is too old to fly the young bird carries her on his back, and supplies her with food:

> "When age had seized and made his dam
> Unfit for flight, the grateful young one takes
> His mother on his back, provides her food,
> Repaying thus her tender care of him
> Ere he was fit to fly."

But here, I am afraid, we are straying into the realms of fiction. While there is hardly room to doubt that the devoted bird at Delft yielded up its life in preference to deserting its young- an act of maternal solicitude which would be equaled by many a little bird in the hedgerows,- or that it watched faithfully by the side of its wounded mate, we must look with suspicion on a stork carrying its infirm old parent about like a Kaffir with a piccaninny on her hips.

Such stories as these have, no doubt, served to strengthen the Eastern belief in the stork as a bird of good augury; but there are passages in the Armenian song referred to above which seem to show that, like the swallow, the bird is welcomed more particularly as a harbinger of spring. "Thou hast brought us the signs of spring" is very suggestive of this idea, as

SUPERSTITIONS ABOUT ANIMALS

are also two verses descriptive of the change of weather which followed the stork's return to a warmer climate:

> "When thou away didst go,
> Away from this tree of ours,
> The withering winds did blow.
> And dried up all the flowers.
> Dark grew the brilliant sky.
> Cloudy and dark and drear;
> They were breaking the snow on high.
> And winter was drawing near."

"Swift-winged and pleasing harbinger of spring," a title given by a Yorkshire poet to the Swallow, gives us a clue to the peculiar veneration in which these birds are universally held. By the ancients they were placed among those requiring special honor, the Romans believing that the spirits of departed children took up their abode in the bodies of these graceful birds, and in this way came periodically to visit their old homes. But this pretty myth only helps to strengthen the supposition that it is as 'a harbinger of spring' that the swallow obtains its title of a bird of good augury, and this belief is implanted deep in the hearts of even little children. Dryden tells us that "Swallows are unlucky birds to kill," and Pope that "Children sacred held a Martin's nest;" and any schoolboy, though perhaps he may not be able to give a reason for his belief, will tell us that to destroy a swallow's nest will bring 'bad luck.'

Among young people the ancient fable which tells us why;

> "Progne makes on chimney-tops her moan.
> And hovers o'er the palace once her own,"

...can have no influence over their feelings; nor in

SUPERSTITIONS ABOUT ANIMALS

England is the swallow, as it is in Sweden, associated in any way with the Crucifixion of our Lord. In addition to believing that bad luck will result from killing a swallow or destroying its nest, many people believe that precisely the reverse will obtain if swallows build under their eaves, and very great care is taken to prevent the birds from being frightened or molested. There is a passage in Hood which seems to refer to this belief:

> "But bid the sacred swallow haunt his eaves
> To guard his roof from lightning and from thieves."

While touring in Turkey some years ago, I was very much interested in a pair of swallows which had the temerity to build a nest on a bracket inside a coffee-house near Constantinople. The bracket, which was not more than seven feet from the ground, had apparently been placed on the wall for the birds' special benefit, and they showed their appreciation by treating the host and his customers as confidential promoters of the scheme. The swallows left and entered the apartment by means of the doorway, which was also used by the customers,' and so little did they fear 'the unspeakable Turk,' that they frequently passed close to his face when they happened to meet him coming in or going out. The presence of the birds seemed to give the proprietor immense satisfaction, and I have no doubt he would stoutly have prevented their receiving any molestation; but whether he considered them harbingers of 'good luck' I cannot say.

Yet while it is not every one who desires to have swallows nesting on their buildings, chiefly in consequence of the dirt which is made by the birds and their young, there are very few people who would wantonly break their nests or frighten them away. "When they go they take your luck away with them," is a common saying. Not more than a few months ago I was told about a farmer who had destroyed a number of swallows' nests on his house and barns, ever since which time the swallows had refused to colonize on his farm buildings, and he had experienced a series of misfortunes. Whether the original builders of a nest which has been destroyed will return at another season to the place of the depredation seems to be somewhat a moot question. I have known of nests remaining in a broken state for many summers after they have been destroyed, the swallows apparently refusing, through fear or vexation, to rebuild the old habitations. That sometimes swallows will repair old nests which have ruthlessly been damaged has been amply proved, but it is very doubtful whether the birds have been the same as those which built them in the first instance. While;

> "The martin and the swallow
> Are God Almighty's bow and arrow,"

It is also said that:

> "The robin and the wren
> Are God Almighty's cock and hen;"

And nothing but ill fortune would attend the callous man who dared to do an injury to our pugnacious little friend the Redbreast, and his tiny wife Jenny Wren.

> "Him that harries their nest,
> Never shall his soul have rest,"

...Says a popular rhyme. Another tells us that:

> "If you go to catch a robin.
> You will come back a-sobbing."

Or in similar words:

SUPERSTITIONS ABOUT ANIMALS

"The red on the breast of a robin that's sought,
Brings blood to the snarer by whom it is caught;"

...or still further:

"A robin in a cage
Sets all heaven in a rage."

Truly, a 'robin in a cage' is a rare as well as an unnatural and disagreeable sight. I shall not soon forget the displeasing impression made upon my own feelings, and upon those of many others, on seeing a robin imprisoned in a pretty painted cage in a side-show. The bird seemed altogether out of place- a little martyr, a fluffy, pathetic appeal to our tenderest natures. Yet, why so more than any other bird 'fastened and imprisoned behind bars'" Can it be that the melancholy fate of the 'breast burned bird' told in the tales of our childhood still linger with us and bring forth our compassion? If so, long may they linger and create sympathies and tender feelings which in these days are all too rare. Happily the pretty redbreast, stained with the blood of our Redeemer (so fables tell us), is yet to be seen in our crofts and on our window-sills, and the appearance of the pugnacious little visitor in our rooms is accepted both as a sign of confidence in our goodwill and an augury of good fortune.

The Cuckoo- "Darling of the spring," as Wordsworth endearingly calls it, is another bird whose name is synonymous with good luck, and this very probably because, like the swallow and the stork, its appearance is significant of spring's sweet advent.

"Hark, how the jolly cuckoos sing
'Cuckoo!' to welcome in the spring."
-John Lyly.

SUPERSTITIONS ABOUT ANIMALS

Whatever you may wish, folks say, when first you hear the cuckoo's call, your wish will be gratified. But a very ancient tradition insists that in order to obtain good luck, especially in affairs of love, it is necessary to hear the notes of the nightingale first. To go back only to the days of Chaucer, we learn:

> "How lovers had a tokening,
> And among hem it was a commune tale
> That it were good to here the nightingale
> Rather than the leud cuckow sing.'"

And the poet tells how, half-asleep and half-awake:

> "I hearde sing
> The sorry bird, the leud cuckow.
> And that was on a tree right fast by,
> But who was than evill apaid but I?
> 'Now God,' quod I, 'that died on the crois,
> Yeve sorrow on thee, and on thy leud vois.
> Full little joy have I now of thy cry.'
>
> And as I with the cuckow thus gan chide,
> I heard in the next bush beside
> A nightingale so lustely sing
> That with her clere voice she made ring
> Through all the greene wood wide.
>
> 'Ah, good nightingale,' quod I then,
> 'A little hast thou ben too long hen.
> For here hath ben the leud cuckow,
> And songen songs rather than hast thou,
> I pray to God evill fire her bren.'"

Milton, in his 'Ode to the Nightingale,' referring to the same superstition, writes:

SUPERSTITIONS ABOUT ANIMALS

"O nightingale, that on yonder blooming spray
Warblest at eve, when all the woods are still:
Thou with fresh hopes the lover's heart dost fill,
While the jolly Hours lead on propitious May.
The liquid notes that close the eyes of day.
First heard before the shallow cuckoo's bill,
Portend success in love; O if Jove's will
Have linked that amorous power to thy soft lay,
Now timely sing, ere the rude bird of hate
Foretell my hopeless doom in some grove nigh."

Chaucer's reference to the cuckoo as a 'leud bird,' and Milton's condemnation of it as 'a rude bird of hate' arise, no doubt, from its association with unfaithfulness in marriage. Probably its own singular habit of leaving its eggs to be hatched by other birds has been the origin of this association. Chaucer represents the bird as cynical in the extreme in its view of love and matrimony. When the nightingale has so beautifully been singing of the virtues which love engenders, the cuckoo sarcastically observes:

"Nightingale, thou speakest wonder faire,
But for all that is the sooth contraire.
For love is in young folke but rage,
And in old folke a great dotage,
Who most it useth, most shall enpaire."

The cry of the cuckoo is supposed to denote mockery, and one of our old English words having this significance is derived from the Latin word cuculus- a cuckoo. Shakespeare, in the song which closes Love's Labour's Lost, uses the note of the cuckoo to convey this meaning:

"When daisies pied, and violets blue,
And lady-smocks all silver white,

SUPERSTITIONS ABOUT ANIMALS

And cuckoo-buds of yellow hue,
Do paint the meadows with delight,
The cuckoo then, on every tree,
Mocks married men; for thus sings he.
Cuckoo;
Cuckoo, cuckoo: O word of fear,
Unpleasing to a married ear!"

Poor cuckoo! What senseless havoc does man's imagination make of Natural History! Through the construction of a stupid fable the cuckoo's 'jolly voice' becomes 'leud', 'hated', and 'a word of fear.' Still, not so, I hope, to most of us. We listen with a rejoicing sense of approaching summer, with all its full verdure and warmth, as once again the curious voice of the hidden bird rings out. And among the poets, too, the bird is not wanting for friendship. Spenser called it "The merry Cuckow, messenger of spring." John Lyly describes it as "jolly;" Wordsworth 'delights' in the voice of the "blithe new-comer;" and John Logan, the Scotch poet, in a gem of poetry devoted to a eulogy of the bird, hails it as "beauteous stranger of the grove." The poem is so delicate and true to nature that I would like to reprint it here in its entirety; three verses, however, must suffice:

"Hail, beauteous stranger of the grove!
Thou messenger of spring!
Now Heaven repairs thy rural seat.
And woods thy welcome sing.
What time the daisy decks the green,
Thy certain voice we hear;
Hast thou a star to guide thy path,
Or mark the rolling year?
Delightful visitant! with thee
I hail the time of flowers,
And hear the sound of music sweet
From birds among the bowers."

SUPERSTITIONS ABOUT ANIMALS

Similar to the expression of a wish on hearing the cuckoo call is the belief that 'any wish will come true' if made on seeing the first lamb of the season, and there is no reservation in this case about seeing or hearing any other animal first. This wholesale kind of wishing, however, is hardly to be commended, for though it may be lucky for the person expressing the wish, it may be very unlucky for other people. Then it is also said that a piebald or white horse is an animal which brings good luck; but some people add that you must express your wish before you think of its tail, a reservation which makes the act of wishing an impossibility. I can well remember how, when I was a schoolboy, it was our invariable custom to expectorate over our little fingers on seeing a white or piebald horse in order to secure good luck.

From the results up to date I must admit I have not very abundant faith in this particular form of superstition. Perhaps, however, I thought of their tails! A black Cat without a single white hair in its fur is almost universally regarded as a 'lucky animal,' and quite a large number of people keep a black cat for no other reason than to ensure prosperity. Woe be to the foolish person who turns one of these sable augurs from his door; and woe, some people say, to those from whose door the animal turns of its own accord. Quite recently a lady told me with great distress she had lost her cat. "I should not have minded," she said, "but it was perfectly black."

The following instance of superstitious belief in black cats appeared in the March (1903) issue of the 'Badminton Magazine,' the subject of the remarks being Prince Ranjitsinhji:

"The Prince has a great superstition in black cats, and the appearance of one at a shooting gathering serves to convince him in advance of a fine morning plus a fine bag, and singularly enough, it always turns out so. Twice in succession, he claims, has the timely appearance of a black cat been instrumental in winning a county match for Sussex in addition to other occasions."

A superstitious belief in cats, black or otherwise, is of very great antiquity. Among the Egyptians the animals were regarded with the utmost reverence, and their mummified remains, a cargo of which was imported to England not many years ago, are frequently found in the same tombs as their worshipers. In witchcraft and soothsaying cats have always played no unimportant part, and wherever we see a picture or description of a witch's hovel, there too we shall certainly find portrayed her companion in darkness, a black cat.

> "In a dirtie Haire-lace
> She leads on a brace
> Of black-bore-cats to attend her
> Who scratch at the Moone,
> And threaten at noone
> Of night from Heaven to render her."
> -Herrick, "The Hag."

One of the special ingredients in the filthy concoctions with which these hags were supposed to work their villainy was the brains of a black cat. Ben Jonson, in his Masque of Queens, mentions this ingredient in the song sung by the witches:

> "I from the jaws of a gardener's bitch,
> Did snatch these bones and then leaped the ditch:
> Yet I went back to the house again,
> Killed the black cat, and here's the brain."

A well-known superstition existing at the present day is that a very minute species of Spider, commonly known as the 'Money-spider' or 'Money-spinner,' will, by creeping upon one's hand, bring good fortune- for preference a legacy. Even timid

SUPERSTITIONS ABOUT ANIMALS

ladies, who would fall in a faint were any other creeping thing to touch them, will allow the little 'Money-spinner' to crawl upon them with impunity, hoping that by permitting it to do so some form of good luck will ensue.

While writing upon the subject of spiders it will not be out of place to mention the popular belief that to kill a spider will certainly cause rain to fall. I have met with this superstition in several parts of the country. In a small town in the West Riding of Yorkshire not long ago, I saw a youngster intently watching a spider making its way across a pavement, or 'causeway' as it is called in those parts. Presently, when the spider was about to reach a place of safety, the boy raised his foot to crush the little creature, but his nurse, who was quick enough to prevent him, cried out with some alarm, "No, don't kill it, or we shall have rain tomorrow."

SUPERSTITIONS ABOUT ANIMALS

DISTORTED NATURAL HISTORY

"O Lord, how manifold are thy works! in wisdom hast thou made them all: the earth is full of thy riches.

So is this great and wide sea, wherein are things creeping innumerable, both small and great beasts.

The glory of the Lord shall endure for ever : the Lord shall rejoice in his works." -Psalm civ.

Apart from signs and omens, there is a form of superstition which owes its origin largely to ignorance in respect of the animal kingdom. This is a surprising and pathetic fact, for it obviously shows that few people are really interested in the marvelous and beautiful creatures with which God has blessed the earth. To me every creature He has made is an object for wonder and admiration. Like Cowper,

"Cawing rooks, and kites that swim sublime
In still-repeated circles, screaming loud,
The jay, the pie, and even the boding owl
That hails the rising moon, have charms for me."

And I may also add snakes, and toads, and slugs, and black beetles. In each there is much that is marvelous, that is beyond our limited comprehension, and not one atom of which can we design much more create. But how very few there are who take so much interest in the various 'birds of the air and beasts of the field' that they will look into books of natural history to find out what kind of a world they live in!

Much of this superstition is almost as amusing as it is extravagant. We hear, for instance, that a cat has nine lives; that an earwig creeps into people's ears and investigates their brains; that a goatsucker (or night-hawk, night-jar, etc.) sucks milk from goats or cows; that adders are deaf; blind-worms are blind; snakes are slimy, can fascinate, and sting; toads are venomous; and so on, each of which is equal to, if not surpassing, the ridiculed 'annual' of the sea-serpent. And it is chiefly because people take so little interest in the wonders of natural history, and accept in perfectly good faith the stupid theories handed down from their great-grandmothers, that these ancient fables are still credited. A cat, let it be said, has only one life, even though it be a pretty tough one; an earwig has not the least desire to creep into people's ears, and if it got there by accident would be extremely uncomfortable; adders can hear as well as any other kind of snake; blindworms have eyes and can use them in good style; snakes are not slimy- they are dry, and they cannot, in my opinion, fascinate, and assuredly they cannot sting, they bite; and a toad is not venomous. But, in spite of books and lectures on natural history, extravagant stories of the animal kingdom will still hold their ground, because it is so much easier to take things for granted than to inquire for oneself.

Let us take, as an example of popular credulity, the yarns which are told about that best known of all four-footed creatures, our own domestic cat. She is regarded almost universally as an unerring barometer. If she sits with her back to the fire, she lets you know that you must bring out your galoshes and waterproof coats; if she washes over her ears, you must expect sunshine; if she scampers about the garden in a madcap fashion, be prepared for a high wind. As a matter of fact, our feline friend turns her back to the fire for the same reason that our grandmothers wear a shawl- to keep their backs warm; and surely the cleanly creature can attend a little more carefully to her toilet, or show an extra degree of animal spirits, without indicating a change in the state of the weather. But so implicitly do many people believe in a cat's ability to act as a barometer that they will actually consult its attitude and practices before undertaking a journey. On this subject Mr. Louis Wain, the well-known 'cat artist' and authority

SUPERSTITIONS ABOUT ANIMALS

on all feline matters, was recently interviewed by a Great Thoughts representative.

Asked as to whether his study of cats and their ways led him to believe in the theory that they often act as barometers, Mr. Wain vigorously replied, "No, I do not think that because a cat washes her face it will necessarily be a fine day on the morrow." And he proceeded to explain the habit in a way that I had not heard of previously- "I think they do that merely to complete an electrical circuit, for by so doing it generates heat, and therefore a pleasing sensation in the fur."

A terrible charge which is brought against cats in general is that of sucking breath from sleeping infants after the manner of Ben Jonson's bloodcurdling hags. If this charge were true, or there were even doubt about it, then every cat should forthwith be unceremoniously turned out of doors, and branded as an enemy of mankind. But happily there is no truth in the allegation whatever. What actually occurs is this: cats have sometimes been known to lie on the breasts of sleeping babes in order to obtain warmth, and in so doing have unintentionally pressed the breath from the little sleepers' bodies, thereby causing suffocation.

A superstition which is equally untrue, but much more poetical, is that a Toad carries in its head a precious jewel, usually said to be a pearl. John Bunyan was among those who, in days of old, gave this remarkable fable their support. In his apology for his great work, Tie Pilgrim's Progress, he wrote:

"If that a pearl may in a toad's head dwell,
And may be found too in an oyster-shell),
If things that promise nothing do contain
What better is than gold- who will disdain
That have an inkling of it there to look
That they may find it?"

SUPERSTITIONS ABOUT ANIMALS

Shakespeare, in As You Like It, mentions the superstition in the following passage:

"Sweet are the uses of adversity,
Which, like the toad, ugly and venomous.
Wears yet a precious jewel in his head."

It is supposed by many that in writing of the 'precious jewel,' Shakespeare intended to suggest the toad's clear, bright eye, which could indeed very fittingly be described by that term. But it is very evident that Bunyan had no such intention when he referred to the pearl as being "found too in an oyster-shell." It cannot be said of an oyster that it has eyes which can be likened to jewels. I need hardly say that if this old-time superstition were true- that a toad carries in its head a precious jewel- some American magnate would long ago have made a corner in toads.

It is a common idea also that the toad is a venomous creature, and apparently this superstition has been prevalent wherever the toad has existed. From the writings of our poets we can measure the aversion with which this poor batrachian is generally regarded. Beginning with Spenser, we find him speaking of:

"The grieslie tode stoole growne mought I se.
And loathed Paddocks (toads) lording on the same."

In the foregoing passage from Shakespeare we have noticed that the dramatist describes the toad as being "ugly and venomous," and in Richard III. he again refers to it in the words:

"Never hung fouler poison on a toad.
Out of my sight, thou dost infect mine eyes."

And again in King Henry VI. (Part III.): "Marked by the

destinies to be avoided as venom toads."

Pope, in one of his satires, describing the character of a certain 'Sporus,' mentions the toad's alleged habit of spitting venom:

> "At the ear of Eve, familiar toad.
> Half froth, half venom spits himself abroad."

Chatterton also denounces the unfortunate creature: "Ye toads, your venom in my footpath spread;" while Gifford, portraying the jealousy of Weston, uses the toad as an example in a way which is very hard on the reptile:

> "Weston! who slunk from truth's imperious light.
> Swells like a filthy toad with secret spite,
> And, envying the fame he cannot hope.
> Spits his black venom at the dust of Pope.
> Reptile accursed!"

Browning, among more modern poets, in his 'Pied Piper,' also regards the toad as an enemy of mankind:

> "Creatures that do people harm-
> The mole and toad and newt and viper."

Perhaps it is scarcely necessary to say that the supposition that a toad is venomous is quite unwarranted. No reptile, or batrachian, strictly speaking, could be less harmful or more useful than our little friend Bufo. It is true that when molested he exudes from his skin a slimy, acrid substance, which is nauseating to animals that venture to take hold of him, though I have never heard of one being poisoned thereby. And as this exudation is the timid creature's sole means of defense, and as it prevents him receiving more molestation than he already has to put up with, we Can only admire the Providence which bestowed it upon him. I have kept many toads as pets, and have found them to be harmless and interesting, and not wanting in intelligence.

They became so tame that they would feed from my hands, and so soon as they knew they had nothing to fear from being handled and examined in a way which could not have been pleasant, they ceased to exude their glandular secretion. There is a story told of a drunken man who for a wager, in a public-house, chewed a toad's head off and subsequently became dangerously ill. The dirty ruffian! But this mad trick in no way proved that the toad was 'venomous.' The acrid secretion in the toad's skin would be quite sufficient to cause the man's illness. Many another creature which is provided by a good and wise Providence with a peculiar secretion for self-defense would have brought on the same illness if treated in the same disgusting way; not a few beetles and flies could be named among this number.

The idea of a toad spitting venom is, of course, ludicrous, though it is even today a very common belief, especially among children. It has been pointed out to me that the 'venom' of toads may have reference to the viscous secretion on their tongues, by which they lay hold of the insects and other 'small fry' which form their diet. This substance, it is said, when brought into contact with a wound will cause serious illness, and has been known even to result in death. There, however, seems to be nothing in this contention. Not long ago the newspapers told us that a scratch by a cat had caused a man's death, and the bite of a dog, even when the animal was in perfect health, has been known to set up acute blood poisoning. I should be very chary of letting the saliva of any kind of animal come in contact with a cut or sore; but if such happened by accident, and I were in consequence to suffer from blood poisoning, I should not denounce that animal as 'venomous.'

SUPERSTITIONS ABOUT ANIMALS

"It is strange," says the author of the famous Natural History of Selborne, "that the matter with regard to the venom of toads has not yet been settled." This was in 1768. In the minds of naturalists the question, I believe, is now entirely settled, though Frank Buckland regarded the toad as poisonous. But among the mass of people there is still, and I am afraid always will be, a firm-rooted opinion that the toad is a venomous creature, and it is loathed and detested accordingly. Schoolboys pitiless in their treatment of things they dislike- stone it and pelt it as they did ages ago, fearful of going too near it lest it should spit its venom upon them. Probably I stoned it myself when I was a youngster- I hope not!- for I believed it to be an evil and vicious thing; and poor, unoffending, useful little creature, it seems to bear upon it a brand of evil, not a precious jewel, and will be hated and persecuted for evermore.

In White's Selborne there is an interesting entry with reference to the healing of cancer by the application of a toad, though it does not appear that the 'cure' obtained a very widespread popularity. "Several intelligent persons," says White, "both gentry and clergy, do, I find, give a great deal of credit to what is asserted in the papers, and I myself dined with a clergyman who seemed to be persuaded that what is related is matter of fact." But Mr. White, rightly, was very skeptical as to the efficacy of this horrible nostrum, and believed that the woman who claimed to work the 'cancer cures' "finds it expedient to amuse the country with this dark and mysterious relation."

General credence has been given to the theory that toads are able to live for long ages in solid blocks of stone without the possibility of nourishment reaching them. In scientific minds this theory for long enough found acceptance, and today there are many well-informed people who still give it their support. In order to put the popular belief- much more popular then than now- to a thorough definite test, Dr. Buckland, father of the well-known naturalist, deposited twenty-four toads in cells carved out of stone, covered with glass for purposes of inspection. Twelve of the cells were twelve inches by five inches, made in coarse oolitic limestone, and twelve, six inches by five inches, in compact siliceous sandstone, the former being so porous as to be easily permeable by water, and probably by air, but the latter being very compact. These blocks of stone containing the unfortunate prisoners, twelve of them being large toads and twelve small, were placed in Dr. Buckland's garden beneath three feet of earth on November 26th, 1825. Within thirteen months of this date all the toads in the sandstone and the small toads in the limestone were dead, although the glass in some instances had been cracked, and in one of the cells 'a large assemblage of minute insects' was found. Before the end of the second year all the large toads in the limestone were also dead.

Dr. Buckland also tried the experiment of placing toads in holes cut in the trunk of an apple-tree, with the result that at the end of a year "every one of the toads was dead, and their bodies were decayed."

A few years ago, while excavations were being made in the North of England, a living toad was discovered which apparently must have been entombed for many years in the solid rock. In order that the circumstances might be scientifically investigated and reported upon, the toad was sent to the Rev. Dr. Tristram, F.R.S., to whom I am greatly indebted for a letter giving the features of the report, which he published in the Press at the conclusion of his investigations. "It proved," he says, "that the animal could not have been for very long where it was found. It was a female full of spawn, and in the stomach were various insects, chiefly earwigs and small beetles, and also bits of straw and a small maggot, but no winged insects. It must have fallen down a crevice, and unable to escape (probably having fallen when very small) depended for food on such substances as accidentally fell into the cavity which imprisoned it. It had only partially shed its skin, not having had room to throw it off, and it still adhered to the fore part of the body and the head. It may have been a year or two in the position in which it was found, but it is impossible that it could have existed there much longer. The most important piece of evidence, the cavity itself, was never found."

This interesting statement, together with the above-mentioned experiments, proves pretty conclusively that so-called embedded or imprisoned toads are by some means or other provided with nourishment during their incarceration. But, as in the foregoing case, and in all others that I have heard or read of, the cavity in which the toad is said to have been imprisoned, being either partially or entirely missing, it is almost impossible to refute conclusively the assertion that the toad has been imprisoned for centuries, or to prove that nourishment must have been supplied through some chink or channel. As Dr. Buckland's experiment shows, toads being sluggish creatures, are able, like snakes, to live without any sort of food for several months; but the experiment also clearly shows that they cannot live beyond this time entirely excluded from air and food.

It is an outrage on one's reason to be asked to believe that any creature can exist for century upon century embedded in the solid rock hundreds of feet below the surface of the earth. Still, the ancient supposition has, even now, numerous advocates. Only a few weeks ago I was supplied with detailed information respecting the discovery of a toad found in a limestone quarry in the County of Durham. But in this case, as in all others of a similar kind, only a portion of the cavity was obtained, and no attempt was made to examine the contents of the animal's stomach. Thus the only two methods by which any practical decision could be arrived at were wanting. Yet in this instance we were asked to believe that the toad had existed in its rocky prison without air and without nourishment for, not only hundreds, but thousands of years; whereas there was no real kind of evidence to show that it had been where it was found for more than a few months. An argument used in favor of this toad's entombment- and of many others found under similar conditions- was that it could not have fallen to so great a depth without being killed or very much injured. Yet it is quite possible (as is suggested by Dr. Tristram in the case of the toad sent to him for examination) that in an early stage of its existence it drifted or was carried there, and had crept through a cranny or fissure into the cavity from which it was unable to find a way of returning to liberty. But for popular imagination it is not always necessary that there should even be a cavity. The very fact of finding a toad in a mine or quarry is in itself, to many persons, sufficient ground for the supposition that the animal must have been entombed there for countless ages.

On the other hand, I think the assertion will commend itself generally that there can be no actual proof of the toad's imprisonment in the absence of the whole or any part of the cavity in which the creature is alleged to have been embedded. While writing on the subject of toads, it will not, I think, be out of place to refer to the popular belief- I cannot call it a superstition- that during springtime myriads of small frogs fall from the clouds. The appearance of these hosts of minute creatures in our own country is so common that any person residing near fields may see them for himself. The question is not one as to the creatures being there (as if they were arrayed for another encounter with the mice), but how they get there in such countless numbers. The general impression is that they have descended with a shower of rain, for it is usually after a rainfall that they appear. I have known of their appearing in such a dense mass that they have darkened a road for a quarter of a mile, and passing vehicles have killed them by thousands. But while the sight of myriads of small frogs is by no means uncommon, it is not often that one is able to instance a personal experience of a plague of large frogs. Such has, however, once, and only once, fallen to our lot. It was in Stellenbosch, Cape Colony, where this extraordinary visitation took place, and from a description I gave of it In the Dewsbury District News last year, the details were as follow:

"How they arrived or whence they came was a mystery; but that they had come, and come on some sort of business of their own, was a living reality. It was about midnight when they arrived. The camp was silent in sleep, save for the nasal music of tired troopers or the neighing of horses in the adjacent lines. The first notice I had of their arrival was on being awakened by something cold alighting on my face. As I raised my hand to find out what the clammy object was, it quickly departed, and I was just about to turn over for another sleep, thinking I had perhaps been mistaken, when one of the troopers cried out: 'Here, chuck it!'

'What's up?' asked the man sleeping next to him, who apparently had received a prod in the ribs. 'Don't go working your arms about like a blooming signaler,' replied the other man gruffly.

'I never moved my arms,' was the reply.

'Yes, you did; you hit me on the face, and don't do it again.'

At this moment another voice chimed in:

'Don't act the goat when a man's asleep.'

'Who's touching you?' was the query which came in a

sleepy voice from the same part of the tent.

'You threw a lump of candle. I felt it hit me on the face, and it's a daft joke to play after ' lights out."

'I swear I was asleep until you awoke me,' was the reply. Then there arose the sound of scuffling, and a voice in some alarm cried out: 'Strike a light, some of you. There's some beastly reptile in the tent. I felt it crawl across my face.'

At once a candle was lighted, and a strange spectacle met our eyes; the tent was alive with frogs. They were squatting on the boxes, on the saddlery, on our rugs and coverings. Frogs everywhere! As we sprang from the ground the little reptiles began to leap about wildly in their excitement to escape, and boots and mess-tins and odds and ends of accouterments were soon flying in all directions. Not for long enough did we get rid of our nocturnal visitors, but where they went to we could not discover, as there was no water near by. Their appearance and disappearance always remained a mystery. Many times subsequently I noticed that after a shower of rain each pool would be alive with croaking frogs, and I have seen tadpoles swimming about in a bowl outside a tent, though the bowl was empty and without animal life a little while previously."

My nocturnal visit from this army of full-grown frogs was more humorous than surprising, though there certainly was an element of mystery in the spasmodic way in which they appeared and disappeared, and my inability to remember whether their advent was signalized by one of those swift deluges of rain which are characteristic of South Africa makes the circumstances still more mysterious. But the presence of innumerable loud-voiced frogs in pools quickly formed by heavy showers of rain was of very common occurrence, and my attention was more fixed on the harmonious chorus they made-some snapping like castanets, others tolling like bells- than how they congregated. My own impression, now that I have thought more of the matter, is that the frogs were scattered about the Karroo previous to the downfalls, and assembled in the pools as they were formed. My attention was naturally attracted to the animals only when they were gathered together, and even then I probably should not have noticed them save for their vocal performances.

The case of the tadpoles is, however, quite of a different kind. Here we had, after a rainfall, the appearance of numerous little creatures in a vessel which previously stood empty. That they were unable to struggle over the ground and leap into the vessel was unquestionable; but it was also unquestionable that they had got into the vessel, and no one was sufficiently interested in them to place them there. I could not do otherwise than believe that they had descended with the rain, though I did not, as I should have done, examine the ground near by to ascertain whether or not other tadpoles had fallen besides those in the tin. Here, then, is a mystery worth unraveling. It is a well-authenticated fact that volcanic dust is carried thousands of miles from an eruption and suspended in the air for as long as three or four months. Is it not possible for tadpoles in their very early stage of existence to be taken into the air and subsequently released and brought to earth with a downfall of rain?

The preposterous story that Salamanders are able to live in fire was at one time commonly accepted as an ordinary fact of natural history, and seeing that naturalists themselves were not certain whether to give the reptiles credit for this remarkable power, or throw it aside with many other stupid notions which had been handed down from Aristotle and Pliny, it was little wonder that unenlightened persons accepted it with implicit faith. Fire was supposed to be the natural element of salamanders, as natural as water is to a fish.

SUPERSTITIONS ABOUT ANIMALS

"As if their wisdoms had conspir'd
The salamander should be burned,
Or like those sophists, that would drown a fish."

It was believed that they were engendered by terrific
heat just as chickens are hatched by the warmth of the hen's
body. But not only were the creatures presumed to be impervious
to heat and actually brought to life in furnaces, they were also
credited, with the power of quenching flames by merely being
brought in contact with them. Quackery was even going to the
extreme of creating schemes by which salamanders might be
brought into the service of mankind as fire-engines. And so
devotedly did the common people cling to these monstrous
fables, upheld in their belief by the credulity of early naturalists,
that it was not until repeated experiments had been made with
the unfortunate reptiles that the superstitions were completely
exposed, and folk settled down to believe they had hitherto
accepted the wildest nonsense as 'gospel truth.' Still the ancient
belief is not altogether dead. The salamander is yet to many
people 'the creature that lives in flames,' and articles of domestic
utility such as 'salamander wool,' a kind of asbestos, and 'the
salamander,' a poker-like article for stimulating fires, help to
keep the old superstition alive.

An experiment, such as I have alluded to for testing the
salamander's imperviousness to heat, is vividly described in John
Wesley's Survey of the Wisdom of God in Creation, an
exhaustive and clever, though, of course, unreliable natural
history, contemporary with Goldsmith's. Mr. Wesley, in writing
of the salamander, says that there is no ground for the belief that
it is able to live in fire, yet at the same time asserts that
salamanders are to be found "near furnaces where the heat is so
great that no other animal could endure it without being
destroyed in a few minutes." But the eminent divine makes no
attempt to give a reason for his assertion, nor does he give one

instance to prove it. He then goes on to describe an experiment which was made by several interested gentlemen to discover whether it was a fact that salamanders could 'really live in fire.'

"Some charcoal," he says, "was kindled and the animal laid upon the burning coals. Immediately it emitted a black liquor which entirely quenched them. They lighted more coals, and laid it upon them. It quenched them a second time in the same manner. But being presently laid on a fresh fire it was in a short time burned to ashes." Little wonder, poor creature! From this description it would seem that Mr. Wesley had rejected one ridiculous story to accept another equally stupid and void of truth. It is quite probable that the description is exaggerated beyond all likeness to the actual experiment. At the same time, it is by no means improbable that a salamander, or for that matter a frog, a toad, or indeed any creature having a glandular secretion in the skin, might be able to endure an exceptional measure of heat much in the same way as one is able to pick up hot substances with the fingers by simply wetting them.

The fear and disgust with which people regard all kinds of creeping things, without respect to their nature or usefulness, is exemplified by the remarkable aversion that is shown to the harmless common Newt. Needless to say, these little batrachians, many of which I have found most interesting pets, are incapable of inflicting the least injury, and hold a very useful and necessary position in the animal kingdom. When Ceres wished to punish the impudent youth who made merry over her consumption of barley water she transformed him into a newt, so that he might be regarded with aversion, but have 'no great power of doing injury.' Still, harmless as the newt is, I can well remember my feeling of terror when, as a child, I passed near a green-covered duck-pond, which, I was told, was full of newts, or efts, that were 'poisonous.' I thought they would jump out and sting me, and I ran past the pond as quickly and as far from it as I possibly could. Yet these people, whose ignorance had been the means of creating this childish terror, were country-bred, descendants of country stock, and had lived all their lives within a stone's-throw of the duck-pond. The fear of these harmless creatures is, however, of very ancient date. We may gather this from a passage in A Midsummer Night's Dream:

> "Newts and blindworms do no wrong,
> Come not near our fairy queen."

As also from two lines in the Faerie Queene, in which Spenser writes of:

> "These marishes and myrie bogs.
> In which the fearful! ewftes do build their bowres."

And coming down to modern times, we find in a quotation which I have already given from the 'Pied Piper of Hamelin' that the newt is mentioned among 'creatures that do people harm.' It will be noticed from Spenser's use of the word 'ewftes' how the modern word 'newt' has gradually evolved from the Anglo-Saxon 'efete'- an 'efete,' an 'ewfte,' an 'ewt,', 'a newt.' In the same way we get the word 'adder'- 'a neddre,', 'an eddre,', 'an adder.'

It is within comparatively recent years that people in country districts, when suffering from indigestion, frequently attributed their abdominal pains to the presence of a newt which they had swallowed in its egg stage. Illness in cattle they sometimes put down to the same reason, and extraordinary means were adopted to get rid of the pest. Indeed, it is quite open to question whether the supposed malady was any worse than the prescription resorted to for the working of 'a cure.' For instance, which may be considered the worse of two evils- to give permanent board and lodgings to a newt in the 'pit of the stomach' or swallow a roasted mouse to get rid of it? I think I would sooner have the newt, for the newt would, after all, be merely imaginary, whereas there would be no doubt whatever about the mouse. It hardly need be said that such a reptile as a newt could not live for more than a few minutes in the human stomach. There have, however, been cases where parasites several inches in length have been brought up, and it is highly probable that these have given rise to the old superstition about newts.

The supposition that Chameleons live on air is of very great antiquity and almost universal. That it dates back to the days of Moses seems almost certain, for among the unclean creeping things mentioned in the book of Leviticus is one which is translated from a word meaning 'to breathe,' and in the Revised Version is rendered 'chameleon.' This reference to breathing leaves no room to doubt that the ancient writer was conversant with the common superstition of his day; and even at the present time the antiquated superstition is implicitly believed in. As one might expect, poets have made free use of this pleasing fancy both for illustration and ornament. Shakespeare, in Hamlet, uses it in the former sense:

"King: How fares our cousin Hamlet?
Hamlet: Excellent, i' faith: of the chameleon's dish: I eat the air promise crammed: you cannot feed capons so."

Charles Churchill, in his humorous satire depicting the stagnation which was to fall on Scotland, writes: "No living thing, whate'er its food, feasts there. But the chameleon who can feast on air."

Shelley, comparing the chameleon with the poet, says:

SUPERSTITIONS ABOUT ANIMALS

"Chameleons feed on light and air;
Poets' food is love and fame."

The reason why poets choose this light diet, he goes on
to explain, is because they dare not 'stain' their 'heavenly mind',
'with wealth or power,' and, pressing the simile, he continues:

"If bright cameleons should devour
Any food but beams and wind.
They would grow as earthly soon
As their brother lizards are."

In the same poem Shelley also refers to the chameleon's
singular faculty of changing color:

"Would they ever change their hue,
As the light chameleons do.
Suiting it to every ray
Twenty times a day?"

The idea here expressed is that the chameleon changes
its color to suit the hue of its environment. Elsewhere the same
poet, still comparing a chameleon with a lover, mentions the
phenomenon in similar terms:

"As a lover or cameleon
Grows like what it looks upon."

The same belief occurs in a poem on 'The Cameleon,' by
Matthew Prior;

"As the cameleon who is known
To have no colours of his own;
But borrows from his neighbour's hue,
His white or black, his green or blue,"

SUPERSTITIONS ABOUT ANIMALS

Unfortunately for poetic imagination, and, I may add, for the point of a speech delivered recently by a prominent statesman- that a certain member on the other side was like a chameleon, able to alter his color to suit his surroundings- there is no truth in the supposition. It is true that chameleons have the faculty of changing their color very highly developed, but this change is now attributed to the peculiar structure of their skin, influenced by their feelings and moods. And need it be said that whatever be the nature of a poet's food, chameleons require something a little more substantial than air for their sustenance- a juicy fly, or a tiny luscious beetle is more suited to their dietary.

Perhaps no superstition has been more used in illustration than that of the Crocodile shedding tears, and many will doubtless wonder how weeping has become associated with such a vicious and dangerous reptile as the crocodile. As we understand the term now, 'crocodile tears' mean hypocritical lamentations, and it is in this sense that the term is commonly used as a simile. The schoolmaster who tells a trembling youngster that the pain which he is about to suffer under the strokes of a supple cane are as nothing compared with the pain which the schoolmaster himself will suffer, may properly be described as 'crocodile tears.' Or the term can accurately be used in connection with the young heir who weeps at the funeral of a crabbed and cantankerous old relative to whose fortune he is succeeding, while, at the same time, he devoutly blesses Providence for having removed the barrier. It is in this sense that Dryden uses the simile in his play, 'All for Love'. Antony tells how "some few days hence" he will be "contracted in his narrow urn," and Octavia, bearing the 'cold ashes' in her "widowed hand to Caesar,",

> "Caesar will weep, the crocodile will weep,
> To see his rival of the universe
> Lie still and peaceful there."

SUPERSTITIONS ABOUT ANIMALS

Sir John Suckling, describing the falseness of a lady, employs the simile:

"Hast thou marked the crocodiles weeping
Or the foxes sleeping?
...Oh ! so false, so false is she!"

Tennyson in his pathetic poem, 'The Dirge,' describing the 'ravings' of the world about one who has finished the 'long day's work' and turned to rest, says:

"Crocodiles wept tears for thee;
The woodbine and eglatere
Drip sweeter dews than traitor's tear.
Let them rave."

This idea of the weeping crocodile, which is now so effectively used to describe humbug and hypocrisy, is founded on an actual belief. In the Middle Ages, travelers returned from foreign climes with the astounding' information that crocodiles, when wishful of luring human beings to destruction, beguiled them with profuse lachrymation, and then consumed them with the same manifestations of sympathy and regret. Bacon definitely alludes to this belief when he says: "It is the wisdom of crocodiles that shed tears when they would devour."

And Shakespeare has in his mind the same wild story when he makes Queen Margaret say:

"Henry, my lord, is cold in great affairs.
Too full of foolish pity, and Gloucester's show
Beguiles him as the mournful crocodile
With sorrow snares relenting passengers."

This extraordinary fabrication, which bears on the very

face of it the imprint of a mere traveler's yarn, was received by the credulous people of those days with the utmost implicitness. In the same way they accepted the absurd stories of 'legless Birds of Paradise' which 'lived on morning dew' and fragrant spices.

> "Those golden birds that, in the spice-time drop
> About the gardens, drunk with that sweet food
> Whose scent hath lur'd them o'er the summer flood.
> And those that under Araby's soft sun
> Built their high nests of budding cinnamon."

And likewise they swallowed the equally stupid yarn, similar to that of the crocodile, that Hyenas cry like children in order to lure sympathetic people to destruction.

> "All night, the lean hyaenas their sad case
> Like starving infants wailed."

It is curious that another old-time error is strengthened by Biblical reference- that a Snail wears itself away by its own motion. "As a snail which melteth," wrote the Psalmist, "let every one of them pass away."

The supposition, it is perhaps hardly necessary to emphasize, is quite inaccurate, but if we accept it as a beautiful metaphor it admirably expresses the Psalmist's meaning. In a book of Scriptural Natural History, published in 1835, I recently came across the following choice morsel of information written in all seriousness upon this subject:

"This reptile (i.e., the snail) lodges in a winding shell and marks out its path with slime. It, therefore, wastes itself away by its own motion, every movement leaving part of its moisture behind." This singular quotation scarcely needs, I think, any comment. Had the writer taken the least trouble to verify his statement by actual observation he would not have committed so glaring and stupid a blunder. How different is the explanation of the Psalmist's metaphor, given by Dr. Tristram in his clever and entertaining Natural History of the Bible: "In order to prevent the evaporation of the moisture of the body all these mollusks which have a thin or semitransparent shell secrete themselves in dry weather... But notwithstanding the care they take to secrete themselves, the heat often dries them- up, either by a long continued drought, or by the sun's rays penetrating to their holes. Thus we find in all parts of the Holy Land myriads of snail shells in fissures, still adhering by the calcareous exudation round their orifice to the surface of the rock, but the animal of which is utterly shriveled and wasted- 'melted away,' according to the expression of the Psalmist."

And now we come to Snakes ! And when I enter upon this part of my subject I am at an utter loss where to begin and where to end, for there is no other creature on the face of the earth of which so little is known and of which so much nonsense is spoken and written. Even the most educated people of the present day ascribe to snakes, or 'serpents,' all sorts of ridiculous powers and functions which the reptiles have never possessed, and slander them in a scurrilous way, that, even to snakes, is more than unkind. Snakes are regarded almost, perhaps I may say altogether, universally with the most intense loathing and fear; and it is no doubt on this account that they have become the objects of more superstition than any other creature. This antipathy is due in a very large measure, I have no doubt, to the curse pronounced upon the Serpent by the Creator after the downfall of our first parents:

"Thou art cursed above all cattle, and above every beast of the field; upon thy belly shalt thou go, and dust shalt thou eat all the days of thy life. And I will put enmity between thee and the woman, and between thy seed and her seed; it shall bruise thy head, and thou shalt bruise his heel."

And speaking of the last things which shall come to pass, St. John, in his marvelous Revelation, describes the seizing and binding of 'that old serpent which is the Devil,' an expression of the deepest loathing and contempt. When Christ uttered his condemnation of the Pharisees his invective culminated in the words "Ye serpents, ye generation of vipers," knowing precisely what the simile would convey to his hearers. But this hatred of the 'serpent tribe' does not appear to have been displayed before the Downfall. We are told that "the serpent was more subtle than any beast of the field," but by this we are not to understand that it was more wicked, simply wiser- "Be ye, therefore, wise as serpents."

It is evident that Eve was on the most comfortable terms with the reptile which was to wreak so much havoc in the blessedness of Paradise, and she seemed to think it nothing out of the ordinary when the Serpent sidled up to make some confidential references to the Tree of Knowledge. Still this is not to be wondered at, if we accept as literal the description of the reptile sketched by Milton in his Paradise Lost. In the first place the reptile was not 'creepy' or 'crawly.' He did not, so Milton tells us, approach her:

> "With indented wave
> Prone on the ground as since."

Quite otherwise, he came towards her 'on his rear,' by which we may suppose that his progression was 'on end' or upright like an ordinary mortal, whose attitude for the moment he was, no doubt, wishful to imitate. But, beyond this, there is another reason why Milton's Serpent struck no terror into the heart of our first mother. Anticipating in Eve's character, it would seem, that love of color and ornament which has been the predominant feature of all her daughters whatever their station, Satan arrayed himself to suit her taste and fancy. It was not as a dull-colored, snaky, objectionable reptile he approached her. Satan knew his quarry. On he came;

> "His head
> Crested aloft, and carbuncle his eyes;
> With burnished neck of verdant gold, erect
> Amidst his circling spires, that on the grass
> Floated redundant: pleasing was his shape,
> And lovely; never since of serpent kind
> Lovelier."

Poor Eve! But even if we suppose that the blind poet had been taxing his imagination for so vivid and fine a description of Eve's betrayer, there is no doubt that from the Genesis account of the Temptation we may understand that Eve did not regard the reptile with aversion. This fearlessness had, however, changed to terror in the days of Pharaoh the persecutor of Israel. When the Lord told Moses to cast his rod upon the ground, and, as a consequence of his action, it became a living serpent, "Moses fled from before it," and man has fled from before it ever since.

A few weeks ago, a singular example of this detestation and fear of snakes was brought to light at an inquest in the East End of London on the body of a poor bedridden youth, who was said to have died from fright on seeing a snake by his bedside. The evidence of the mother and other witnesses very clearly showed how exaggerated statements respecting snakes have become popular belief. Not only did they describe the reptile as being very much larger than it actually was, but they also gave lurid descriptions of its flashing eyes and glittering fangs, and the picture was made more realistic, if inaccurate, by a neighbor explaining how she fed the angry creature with pieces of bread to keep it quiet! Unfortunately for the veracity of the witnesses, the naturalist from whom the reptile had escaped was able to prove that it was only a harmless English grass-snake not more than two feet long, and therefore quite devoid of poisonous 'fangs.'

Arising out of this fear of the reptiles, and a marked inaccurate knowledge of their nature and habits, serpents were, in days of old, objects of great veneration, and the most absurd traditions were created in respect of their size and power. Only one or two of these need be mentioned to give an idea of the terrible nature of the reptiles which ancient imagination conjured up. At the Siege of Troy, two monstrous serpents came up out of the sea and killed Laocoon, the high priest of Apollo, and his two sons. According to Diodorus, the Sicilian, an Egyptian snake, measuring thirty cubits long, was captured and brought to Alexandria. While Regulus was with his army near Carthage, a terrible serpent stopped their advancement on the banks of the river Begrada, and made a meal of a large number of his soldiers before the reptile was put to death by a stone from a catapult.

Whenever a writer, be he ancient or modern, sits down to describe a snake, or 'serpent' as he prefers to call the reptile, he seems to delight in letting his imagination have free scope in depicting a creature terrible in aspect, impossible in architectural construction, and omnivorous in tastes. Thus Virgil (Dryden's rendering) describes a serpent which crept from Anchises' tomb:

> "His huge bulk on sev'n high volumes roll'd;
> Blue was his breadth of back, but streak'd with scaly gold:
> Thus riding on his curls, he seem'd to pass
> A rolling fire along, and singe the grass.
> More various colors through his body run
> Than Iris when her bow imbibes the sun.
> Betwixt the rising altars, and around,
> The sacred monster shot along the ground;

SUPERSTITIONS ABOUT ANIMALS

With harmless play amidst the bowls he pass'd.
And with his lolling tongue assay'd his taste:
Thus fed with holy food the wondrous guest
Within the hollow tomb retir'd to rest."

And undertaking the description of a snake (the one referred to above was a serpent) the same poet writes:

"So shines, renew'd in youth, the crested snake.
Who slept the winter in a thorny brake.
And, casting off his slough when spring returns.
Now looks aloft, and with new glory burns,
Restor'd with pois'nous herbs : his ardent sides
Reflect the sun; and, rais'd on spires, he rides
High o'er the grass; hissing, he rolls along.
And brandishes by fits his forky tongue."

Thus we are given to understand that whilst both serpent and snake roll and ride, the serpent also has the faculty of shooting. And, whereas the serpent who lived in Anchises' tomb laps his food out of 'bowls' with his 'lolling tongue' like a tame mouser, the snake restores his strength, after a winter fast, with 'poisonous herbs.' Truly the reptiles of ancient times must have been wondrous creatures. But now let us turn to a modern poet, and see if we can come any nearer to an accurate description of a serpent. This is what the serpents in Longfellow's 'Hiawatha' look like:

"Soon he reached the fiery serpents,
The Kenabeek, the great serpents,
Lying huge upon the water,
Sparkling, rippling in the water,
With their blazing crests uplifted.
Breathing fiery fogs and vapors.
So that none could pass beyond them."

SUPERSTITIONS ABOUT ANIMALS

True, this is a description of those legendary reptiles which guarded the habitation of Megissogwon, the magician; but in the words 'fiery serpents' we have a distinct reference to the 'fiery flying serpents' of the Old Testament ('fiery' on account of their bite, and 'flying' because of their swift method of striking); and the power of breathing fiery fogs and vapors (surely a paradox) is nothing more than was attributed to the basilisk or cockatrice, which is alleged to have killed vegetation by breathing upon it. Nor indeed is the description more exaggerated than that given by many another author who might be quoted, nor does it exceed anything which a person of ordinary intelligence would write to-day if you were to put pen and paper before him and ask him to give you a faithful description of a common English adder. Snakes always have been, and, I am afraid, always will be, credited with all kinds of wonderful attributes which they do not possess nor ever have possessed, and people seem always ready to believe anything about them which is nasty or inaccurate. For instance, people who have never had the pleasure of handling the reptiles insist that they are 'slimy.' This is a very great mistake, and is as much a slander as if the snakes were to contend that such people never washed themselves. I have handled numerous snakes, but have not yet found one that was 'slimy.' Sometimes they have been cold; but then snakes, being cold-blooded creatures, take their temperature from surrounding objects, so that they cannot be blamed for having a cold skin if they are kept in cold places. The error into which writers have fallen in regard to 'slippery' or 'slimy' snakes is perhaps not to be wondered at considering the natural prejudice against the reptiles, which would preclude a closer acquaintance than was absolutely necessary. Virgil writes of the 'slippery serpent.'

William Seeker says that "Snails leave their slime behind them as well as serpents." Chatterton asserts that "The slimy serpent swelters in its course." Byron goes to the extreme of explaining the actual color of the 'slime':

> "If like a snake she steal within your walls
> Till the black slime betray her as she crawls."

Shakespeare is even more explicit. In the play of Antony and Cleopatra, after the Queen has died from the bite of an asp, one of Caesar's guards, who has made an examination of the apartment, exclaims:

> "This is an aspic's trail, and these fig leaves
> Have slime upon them such as the aspic leaves
> Upon the caves of Nile."

However thrilling and dramatic this finding of the 'aspic's trail' may be, as matter of fact it is an utter violation of the truth. The snake which Cleopatra 'applied to her breast,' after having 'pursued conclusions infinite of easy ways to die,' was very probably the horned cerastes, a deadly reptile which, far from seeking the cool seclusion of the 'caves of Nile,' or any other caves, finds supreme enjoyment in basking in the hottest places it can discover.

"So grateful to the heat is this snake," says Bruce, the celebrated traveler, "that though the sun was burning hot all day, when we made a fire at night by digging a hole and burning wood to charcoal in it for dressing our victuals, it was seldom that we had fewer than half-a-dozen of these vipers, which burned themselves to death by approaching the embers."

The slime on the fig-leaves was assuredly not the trade mark of this dry-skinned reptile, nor was it the 'slime' of any other kind of snake which Cleopatra could obtain. Shakespeare is very true to nature where he has had the opportunity of studying his subject, but he merely expresses the common and erroneous ideas of his day when he comes to deal with snakes.

There is also a general, but false, impression that snakes 'sting.' How often we may hear the remark when a snake thrusts out its delicate forked tongue: "Look! It is putting out its sting!" The supposition evidently is that this organ is charged with poison, and inflicts a wound by penetration. This is true of the 'sting' of a wasp, as I have many times experienced when in my early days I hunted for wasps' nests in the hedgerows round Devonshire orchards; but it is not true of a snake. A snake bites! It uses its teeth, or fangs, much after the manner of a dog- that is, by snapping, and waits for the poison to take effect before consuming its prey. This, of course, is true only of the venomous species.

A constrictor grasps its prey with its teeth, throws its relentless coils round the unfortunate creature, and then swallows it. Other snakes which are neither venomous nor constricting lay hold of their prey with their needle-like teeth, and, never letting go for an instant, work it head-foremost down their gullets. Those few varieties which feed solely upon birds' eggs are provided with spinous processes standing out from the vertebrae, by which the shell of the egg is fractured in its passage, and the contents are thus safely received for digestion and assimilation. But no snake stings! So true is this that I would permit the most venomous snake to lick my hand till further orders, presuming of course that it would not be in a position to make use of its teeth. The impression that a snake uses its tongue to inflict a wound is apparently as ancient as the reptile itself. In the book of Job we find the tongue spoken of as an instrument of death: "The viper's tongue shall slay him."

This, however, in the Bible, is an isolated instance. Most of the sacred writers, apparently well acquainted with the habits of the reptiles they describe, speak of their bite:

SUPERSTITIONS ABOUT ANIMALS

"Behold, I will send serpents, cockatrices, among you, which will not be charmed, and they shall bite you, saith the Lord." -Jeremiah.

"And the Lord sent fiery serpents among the people, and they bit the people; and much people of Israel died." -Numbers.

"At the last it biteth like a serpent, and stingeth like an adder." -Proverbs.

"And when Paul had gathered a bundle of sticks, and laid them on the fire, there came a viper out of the heat, and fastened on his hand." -The Acts.

But among the Ancients the tongue was believed to be the instrument by which death was caused. Ovid mentions it in this respect: "Behold! a snake lurking in the grass, with its barbed sting wounds her foot as she flies, and leaves its venom in her body."

Virgil frequently represents the snake as 'brandishing her tongue,' or 'brandishing his forky tongue,' as if that were the weapon by which it injected its poison, and he uses the word 'sting' in association with the same organ: "Beware the secret snake that shoots a sting."

Once he goes so far as to describe two serpents which were both venomous and constricting, and in addition makes them use their teeth as if for the purpose of mastication:

"And first around the tender boys they wind.
Then with their sharpen'd fangs their limbs and bodies grind.
The wretched father running to their aid
With pious haste, but vain, they next invade;

SUPERSTITIONS ABOUT ANIMALS

Twice round his waist their winding volumes roll'd,
And twice about his gasping throat they fold.
The pious priest thus doubly chok'd- their crests divide,
And tow'ring o'er his head in triumph ride.
With both his hands he labours at the knots;
His holy fillets the blue venom blots."

But then these were no ordinary serpents; they lived in
the sea! Chaucer, in his quaint 'Legende of Cleopatras,' attributes
the death of the queen to the stings of serpents. His description
of the careful way Cleopatra arranges her death should be read to
be appreciated. Having embalmed the body of Antony and
fastened it in a shrine, she digs a pit alongside, fills it with
serpents, and, naked, steps among them, and is stung to death:

"And next the shrine a pit than doth she grave,
And all the serpentes that she might have.
She put them in that grave.
And with that word, naked, with full good herte,
Among the serpents in the pit she start,
And there she chose to have her burying.
Anone the neders (snakes) gonne her for to sting,
And she her death receiveth with good chere,
For love of Antony that was her so dere."

Shakespeare, on the other hand, curiously enough makes
this tragic death almost his solitary instance of the bite of a
snake:

"Come thou mortal wretch,
With thy sharp teeth this knot intrinsicate
Of life at once untie; poor venomous fool.
Be angry, and despatch."

In most other instances he refers directly or indirectly to

the tongue as the organ by which poison is introduced. Here are some:

"What, wouldst thou have a serpent sting thee twice?"
-Merchant of Venice.

"Snakes, in my heart-blood warm'd, that sting my heart!"
-King Richard II.

"I fear me you but warm the starved snake
Who cherish'd in your breasts, will sting your hearts."
-King Henry VI. (Part II.).

"An adder did it; for with doubler tongue
Than thine, thou serpent, never adder stung."
-A Midsummer Nights Dream.

"Guard it, I pray thee, with a lurking adder
Whose double tongue may with a mortal touch
Throw death upon thy sovereign's enemies."
-King Richard II.

"Were there a serpent seen, with forked tongue,
That slyly glided towards your majesty,
It were but necessary you were waked,
Lest, being suffer'd in that harmful slumber
The mortal worm might make the sleep eternal."
-King Henry VI. (Part II.).

Spenser uses the word 'stings' when speaking of the asp's power of inflicting a death-wound: "Like the stings of aspes that kill with smart." And Dryden obviously supposes that a snake has a sting in its tongue when he writes that "A serpent shoots his sting."

SUPERSTITIONS ABOUT ANIMALS

Another faculty which snakes are said to possess is that of 'fascination.' Here I am treading on somewhat treacherous ground, for while it is a simple matter to prove that snakes are not slimy, and cannot sting, it would be no easy task to prove that they have not the power to fascinate. In the entertaining Scriptural Natural History from which I have previously quoted, there is an interesting reference to this subject which very clearly illustrates the opinion which was commonly held at that period:

"The black snake is found in America, but it is a harmless creature... Its eyes appear like fire for brightness, by means of which it is said to be capable of fascinating birds who tremble on the wing, and are at length so completely frightened as to fall into the serpent's mouth."

A terrible sort of creature to be creeping about. John Wesley, however, writing at an earlier date, gives a much better idea of the fascination theory: "It is very remarkable," he says, and I cordially agree with him, "that he (the rattlesnake) frequently stays under a tree, on which a bird or squirrel is hopping about, with his mouth wide open. And the event constantly is the creature in a while drops into it."

"A swallow," he goes on to say, "pursuing his prey in the air, if he casts his eye on a Snake beneath him, waiting with his mouth wide open, alters his course, and flutters over him in the utmost consternation, till sinking gradually lower and lower he at last drops into his mouth." Another story which the eminent divine tells about the rattlesnake is even still more extraordinary, and shows that this snake has lost none of that primeval subtlety which distinguished these reptiles from the rest of their fellows:

"The rattlesnake, being less nimble than others, would find difficulty in getting its prey were it not for the singular provision made by the rattle in his tail. When he sees a squirrel or bird on a tree he gets to the bottom and shakes this instrument. The creature, looking down, sees the terrible eye of the snake bent full upon it. It trembles, and never attempts to escape, but keeps its eye upon the destroyer, till tired with hopping from bough to bough, it falls down and is devoured." Numerous other writers, among whom I will mention only Byron and another, tell similar stories respecting this singular faculty of 'fascination,' or use it for the purpose of illustration:

> "And like the bird whose pinions quake.
> But cannot fly the gazing snake,
> Will others quail beneath his look.
> Nor 'scape the glance they scarce can brook."
> -The Giaour.

The other reference is to a tale told of an Indian missionary. Seated on his veranda one day he saw a bird fluttering and trembling near by as if in great terror. He then noticed that the little creature was being transfixed by the gaze of a snake which glided towards it. Rising from his seat he stepped between the snake and its quarry, and thus breaking the spell liberated the bird, which flew happily away.

What explanation can we give for the common belief in this power of fascination? Such stories as those I have mentioned bear unmistakably the imprint of exaggeration, but they serve to show how entirely and credulously educated people have accepted glaring errors respecting the power of serpents. And today this faculty of fascination is as innocently believed in as it was a century or more ago. Such a common belief must have had some reasonable origin. The 'sliminess' of serpents probably originated in their silent, stealthy progression, marvelous and mystical, so it seems, in their total want of limbs. The 'sting,' doubtless, may be traced to the continuous flickering of the forked tongue, which, even when the reptile's mouth is shut, continues its movement. And in some similar way, most probably, the common idea of fascination arose.

We may at once dismiss the statement that birds or squirrels tumble headlong into serpents' yawning mouths, unable to resist their seductive eyes. The idea is altogether too grotesque; but it is possible that, like many other flagrant errors, it had its origin in a matter of fact. Probably the inventive person who set this fable going saw 'a bird or squirrel' struggling on the earth a few feet distant from a snake as if the poor creature were held spellbound, and then saw the snake seize it and swallow it. In this case the animal had already been bitten by the reptile, which merely was waiting for death to ensue, well knowing that its prey had no chance of escape. Another theory of fascination, and one which seems to be most reasonable, is that the reptiles' prey are stricken with abject, numbing terror.

"The sight of a venomous snake," says Figuier, though why necessarily venomous he does not say, "sometimes renders its victims immovable, incapable of flight, and, as it were, paralyzed, in which helpless condition they are seized without opposing the slightest resistance. M. Dumeril, while pursuing experiments in the Museum of Natural History demonstrative of the sudden and mortal action of the bite of a viper on a little bird, saw a goldfinch which he held in his hands die suddenly merely at the sight of one."

I remember some years ago a porter at a London station attempting to cross the railway-line just as an express came thundering into sight not a hundred yards distant. There was time for the man to cross to a place of safety, or get back again to the platform he had left, but he stood rooted, so it seemed, between the lines, staring with horror-stricken eyes at the approaching express, and in a moment was cut to fragments. Could it be said of this man that he was 'fascinated?'

SUPERSTITIONS ABOUT ANIMALS

Another 'snake story' is that before consuming their prey snakes carefully lick them all over, so that, being well lubricated, they will slip down the snakes' gullets more easily. Needless to say this habit is quite imaginary. There is scarcely enough moisture on a snake's tongue to cover a beetle. The idea has arisen from the snakes' habit of investigating their food with their tongues before they swallow it. While on the subject of snakes I cannot do otherwise than say a few words about 'snake-charming,' though I must acknowledge, at the outset, that the subject is one on which I find it difficult to express any definite opinion. I have met with more than one gentleman who has declared that he has seen cobras 'charmed' by Indian natives, and has been quite satisfied with the genuineness of the performance. Others have declared that the reptiles employed by the charmers were invariably deprived of their fangs, had their lips stitched together, or in some other way prevented from striking. In the written statements of eye-witnesses the same difference of opinion may be noted. A Government official in Egypt, who was also a naturalist, discovered some years ago that a so-called horned cerastes, with which the chief snake-charmer was supposed to be doing some marvelous feats, was nothing more dangerous than a common non-poisonous variety upon which artificial horns had been fixed. And it is pretty certain that the pythons with which most traveling charmers entertain the public are kept at such a low temperature as to be wanting of sufficient vitality to constrict. On the other hand. Dr. Thomson, the author of the celebrated work on the Holy Land, declares that he has seen many serpent-charmers who do really exercise some extraordinary power over snakes. The snake charmer, he says, is often required to perform his feats in the full light of day, surrounded by spectators, yet his success is always complete. Dr. Tristram bears out this statement also from personal experience.

"The charmers," he remarks, "are not impostors; for though they may sometimes remove their fangs, it is a. well attested fact that they generally allow them to remain, and they will operate on the animals when just caught as willingly as on individuals which have long been in their possession; but they are very reluctant to make experiments on any other species than the cobra."

The practice of snake-charming is of very great antiquity, and is mentioned by the Psalmist: "They are like the deaf adder that stoppeth her ear; Which will not hearken to the voice of charmers, charming never so wisely."

By-the-bye, what sort of an animal is this celebrated Deaf Adder? In all my investigations into Natural History I have not yet met with a specimen, and if there is one reptile more than another I have a great desire to meet it is this wonderful adder which cannot be charmed. Shakespeare, it would seem, believed in the existence of the reptile, or, at any rate, he thought it a capital specimen for purposes of illustration:

"For pleasure and revenge
Have ears more deaf than adders to the voice
Of any true decision."
-Troilus and Cressida.

"What! Art thou like the adder waxen deaf?"
-King Henry VI.

Many country people of the present day are foolish enough to believe that the harmless, timid blind worm, or slow worm, is the cunning creature of which the Psalmist wrote; and my good friend the naturalist who flourished early in last century can actually describe the creature for us. Hear him!- "It will lay one ear close to the ground and cover the other ear with its tail to prevent itself from hearing the sound of the music."

SUPERSTITIONS ABOUT ANIMALS

The intelligent animal! No wonder it cannot be tamed. Now, what is the simple truth of the matter? We have it in a nutshell. Unimaginative people persist in reading Holy Scripture as if every word were a plain matter of fact. They strip it of every vestige of its beautiful warmth of coloring and expressive allegory, and puzzle themselves with self-created difficulties which have existence only in their own dull comprehension. The Psalmist never meant it to be understood that such a creature as a 'deaf adder' had a real existence. Such a rendering of the text utterly spoils his simile. He was describing the nature of wicked people, and wished to convey the significant truth that just as some snakes cannot be charmed, so the wicked will not obey the injunctions of God. That is simple enough. The same meaning is contained in one of our own well known proverbs: "There are none so deaf as those who will not hear."

In another verse the Psalmist writes: "Their poison is like the poison of a serpent." Are we then also to believe that wicked people go about with bags of poison in their cheeks? If we accept one figure literally we must deal with the other in the same way. As we have seen from the sacred writers' frequent references to the 'bite' of serpents, while so many modern writers mention the words 'sting' and 'tongue,' the natural history of the Bible is very true. We cannot improve upon it; though, as we shall notice in the last division of my subject, translators have tried to, by introducing animals which have had no real existence.

Another reptile which crawls abroad under a misnomer is the Blindworm, or Slow worm; a poor, frail, nervous creature, which ignorance tells us is deadly venomous. Shakespeare calls it "the eyeless venom'd worm," and mentions one of the ingredients of the witches' cauldron as being 'a blindworm's sting.' Herrick also believes it to be dangerous:

SUPERSTITIONS ABOUT ANIMALS

"No will-o'-th'-wispe mis-light thee;
Nor snake or slow-worme bite thee."

Scott gives it the character of being slimy and slow:

"There the slow blindworm left his slime
On the fleet limbs that mocked at time."

Here, in these few quotations, we have the common erroneous ideas respecting this frail little reptile. It is popularly supposed to be venomous, eyeless, slow, and slimy, and what is even worse, by country people it is believed to be one of those very creatures which stopped their ears and would not listen to the voice of the charmers. But how utterly unwarranted are these impressions. Not only has a blindworm eyes, but it also uses them with such effect that the little creature vanishes like a flash before you can even get a glimpse of it; a rustle of moss, and it has gone. Thus it is neither a blind worm nor a slow worm. Nor is it venomous; far otherwise. Its tiny teeth are scarcely able to make an impression on one's bare skin, and so nervous is it that when handled it becomes rigid with terror, and can easily be snapped in pieces- hence its name Anguis fragilis.

As for being 'slimy,' all nasty creatures are popularly supposed to be 'slimy'! This, then, is the 'eyeless venom'd worm,' the little creature to whom the fairies sang:

"Newts and blindworms do no wrong.
Come not near our fairy queen "

...a timid, useful reptile which any one might handle without the least repugnance. The reason why it has been misunderstood and misnamed is because its real position in the animal kingdom has not been appreciated. The blindworm is not a worm, or snake, at all. It is, strictly speaking, a lizard; but its limits having become obsolete, its outward appearance in many respects resembles that of a true snake. There is one feature, however, which distinguishes it at once. Like other members of the lizard family, the blindworm has eyelids. In this respect it differs from the true snakes, which, strangely enough, "go about the world with their eyes open," for the very simple reason that they cannot shut them. In consequence of this peculiarity, when blindworms have been found hibernating in the company of snakes, their closed eyes have formed a striking contrast against the wide-open eyes of the other reptiles, and given them the reputation of being blind.

There are numerous other strange superstitions about snakes in general which show how little their real nature is understood. One of these yarns is that, however much they may be injured, they cannot die until the sun goes down. That this is untrue I have proved by killing them in the forenoon and carrying them home in my pockets. The most probable explanation of this stupid belief is that snakes possess so much vitality that unless the backbone is actually broken they will sometimes remain slowly dying until darkness has set in. In the morning they will, of course, be found to have died, giving the impression that, as the superstition has it: "they were waiting for the sun to set."

Equally strange and untrue, it is scarcely necessary to say, is the assertion that if a snake be cut in pieces, no matter how far the bits are separated, they will rejoin, and the snake will live on happily as if nothing had happened. Nor is it less stupid to believe, as many country people do, that if you go to sleep in the open a snake will creep down your throat. What with crows, and earwigs, and snakes, tramps must find sleeping in hedgerows very inconvenient. Shakespeare refers to this superstition in As You Like It:

SUPERSTITIONS ABOUT ANIMALS

"Under an oak, whose boughs were moss'd with age,
And high top bald with dry antiquity,
A wretched ragged man, o'ergrown with hair,
Lay sleeping on his back; about his neck
A green and gilded snake had wreathed itself,
Who with her head nimble in threats approach'd
The opening of his mouth."

Of the extreme virulence of snake poison many wonderful stories are told, and if we accept one in every hundred as being fairly accurate we shall not be unduly misled. Here is a sample. An American farmer, while working in his fields in the heat of a summer noonday, was attacked by a huge rattlesnake, which endeavored to fix its fangs in the farmer's leg. To repulse the attack, the farmer began to lay about him with the rake, and the snake, seeing that a bite of the leg was out of the question, seized the rake with its fangs and severely bit it. "When, lo! in a moment," explained the American farmer, "the wood of the rake swelled to an enormous size!" This is an American story, and is given in evidence of what a rattlesnake can do when it seriously sets to work.

But it is left to an Englishman to give the most effective illustration of the terrible nature of a rattlesnake's venom. If we are at all dubious about the truth of the American snake story, what shall we say of the following' yarn given with all seriousness in A Survey of the Wonders of God in Creation:

"Of how extremely penetrating a nature is their poison? A man provoking one of them to bite the edge of his broad ax, the color of the steel part presently changed: and at the first stroke he made with it in his work, the discolored part broke out leaving a gap in the ax." How thankful English farmers should be that there are no rattlesnakes in England!

SUPERSTITIONS ABOUT ANIMALS

The much debated question as to whether a viper gives refuge to her progeny down her own throat when danger threatens them is, I believe, still awaiting definite settlement. Much has been said on behalf of the supposition by people who affirm they have seen a viper in the act of concealing her young in this extraordinary manner. But the only means of solving the problem- capturing a viper with the young inside her- has not yet, so far as I have been able to ascertain, been carried out. Under these circumstances, it would be manifestly unfair to write of this alleged curiosity of nature as a mere superstition. By this time, I think, my readers will have become tired of reading about snakes, a subject which, I know, has a fascination for only a very few people.

Let us therefore turn to other superstitions which will make pleasanter reading for the majority. A very extraordinary supposition, and one which it is difficult to treat seriously, is that the Swallow, 'the swift-winged and pleasing harbinger of spring,' passes away the cold months of winter at the bottom of a pond or river. Yet this was at one time no isolated opinion. Pepys was not the only one who believed that "Swallows are often brought up in nets out of the mud from under water, hanging together to some twig or other dead in ropes and brought to the fire will come to life."

Dr. Johnson held the same opinion as the dear old gossiper, though he does not go quite so far as to say that the birds were dead. "Swallows," he says, "certainly sleep all winter. A number of them conglobulate together by flying round and round and then, all in a heap, throw themselves under water and lie in the bed of a river."

It is not easy to understand how so strange and unnatural a belief became common. The most probable reason is that swallows, when chasing their natural food- gnats, flies, and kindred insects- approach so near to the surface of rivers and ponds as to 'skim' the water now and again. Their disappearance at the period of migration, added to the foregoing habit, would be sufficient to give rise to the belief that, in order to escape the wintry blasts and frosts, they dived beneath the water and lay dormant in the mud.

The supposition that swallows spend the winter months in England in a state of torpor, instead of seeking warmer climes, was at one time generally accepted as a matter of fact. Gilbert White, while declaring that he had never heard an account of alleged torpidity 'worth attending to,' supports the theory that many swallows remain during the winter months in 'holes and caverns.'

"I am more and more induced to believe," he writes, "that many of the swallow kind do not depart from this island, but lay themselves up in holes and caverns; and do, insect-like and bat-like, come forth at mild times, and then retire again to their latebrae."

He, however, gives some very interesting examples of the popular superstition of his day. "A clergyman of an inquisitive turn," he writes, "assures me that when he was a great boy some workmen, in pulling down the battlements of a church tower early in the spring, found two or three swifts (Hirundines apodes) among the rubbish, which were at first appearance dead, but on being carried to the fire revived. He told me that out of his great care to preserve them he put them in a paper bag, and hung them by the kitchen fire, where they were suffocated. Another intelligent person has informed me that while he was a schoolboy at Brighthelttistone in Sussex (the early name of Brighton) a great fragment of the chalk cliff fell down one stormy winter on the beach, and that many people found swallows among the rubbish."

SUPERSTITIONS ABOUT ANIMALS

Mr. White then goes on to say: "But on my questioning him whether he saw any of those birds himself, to my no small disappointment, he answered me in the negative; but that others assured him they did." How like many other strange stories that get abroad! He had not seen the swallows, but he knew others who had.

Several of our poets have preserved for us in verse the hibernation of our feathered visitors. Thomas Carew, as early as the dawn of the seventeenth century, writing on the 'Approach of Spring,' calls the swallow 'dead':

> "But the warm sun thaws the benumb'd earth,
> And makes it tender; gives a sacred birth
> To the dead swallow."

Yet the same poet seems well aware that swallows are annual visitants:

> "Like swallows, when your summer's done.
> They'll fly and seek some warmer sun."

Cowper writes very much after the same manner:

> "The swallows in their torpid state
> Compose their useless wing."

But also says:

> "She comes in the spring, all the summer stays.
> And, dreading the cold, still follows the sun."

Thomson, halting between two opinions, gives the birds the alternative of seeking 'warmer climes' or retiring to 'their wintry slumbers,' where they "In clusters clung, beneath the mould'ring bank, and where, unpierc'd by frost, the cavern sweats."

Dryden seems in a similar predicament. He tells us how the swallow, knowing 'by instinct or prophecy' that winter was approaching, summoned her family to the summit of a steeple, where they held a 'common council,' and decided on flight. Next day, therefore, says the poet;

> "All to the general rendezvous repair.
> They try their fluttering wings, and thrust themselves in air:
> But whether upward to the moon they go.
> Or dream the winter out in caves below.
> Or hawk at flies elsewhere, concerns us not to know."

Yet he adds: "Southwards, you may be sure, they bent their flight."

In another part of the same poem Dryden tells us how a martin and his 'race,' battered by 'rattling hailstones, mixed with snow and rain,' looked about for a place to spend the winter months in, and "Took shelter in a hollow tree;" from which, however, they were soon hustled by a 'sturdy clown' and 'all the rabble of the town.'

> "...because the laws provide
> No martin there in winter shall abide."

Of course the whole poem is a satire, but these extracts show that at the time it was written, the time also when Pepys accepted the yarn about swallows sleeping under water, the common opinion of the people was that the swallow tribe passed away the winter months in a state of torpor. In this country we have no legends about the swallow, but in Sweden it is a bird of some importance, on account of its supposed association with the death of our Lord. There is a legend about it in that country very similar to those of our own pet bird, Robin Redbreast, both of which I shall give in the proper place. In his poem, 'The Swallow,' Leland tells us how:

> "When Jesus hung upon the Cross,
> The birds, 'tis said, bewailed the loss
> Of Him who first to mortals taught,
> Guiding with love the life of all.
> And heeding e'en the sparrows' fall.
> But, as old Swedish legends say,
> Of all the birds upon that day.
> The swallow felt the deepest grief.
> And longed to give her Lord relief,
> And chirped when any near would come,
> 'Hugswala swala swala honom!'
> Meaning, as they who tell it deem,
> Oh cool, oh cool and comfort Him."

In one of Moore's "Odes of Anacreon" we find the two lines:

> "And Progna, hapless, frantic maid.
> Is now a swallow in the shade."

And turning to Dryden's translation of Virgil's 'Pastorals' we meet with the swallow under the same name:

> "While Progne makes on chimney-tops her moan.
> And hovers o'er the palace once her own."

Both these quotations have reference to the same ancient fable, a fable which probably has been more alluded to by our poets than any other. Progne and Philomela were two sisters, daughters of Pandion, King of Athens. Progne was married to Tereus, King of Thrace, for services he had rendered to Pandion. Philomela, who was unmarried, lived with her father. Yearning for the society of her sister, Progne entreats her husband to go to Pandion and ask him to permit Philomela to visit her, even if only for a little while, and Tereus sets sail on his mission. While he is urging his wife's request with King Pandion, Philomela enters richly arrayed, but her personal beauty is even far richer than her apparel. Tereus is overwhelmed by her charms, and adds his own entreaties to those of his wife's. Philomela also pleads to be allowed to go to her sister, and King Pandion, overcome by their importunity, consents. Tereus and Philomela then set sail for Thrace, but soon the evil intentions of Tereus become known to the unfortunate woman. His wicked passion gains the mastery over his honor, and thrusting his sister-in-law into a castle in a lonely wood he takes advantage of her helplessness.

Then, fearful of her betraying his villainy, he tears out her tongue, and returning to Progne tells her with feigned grief that Philomela is dead. But guarded from flight and deprived of the power of speech, Philomela is not without means of making her terrible condition known to her sister. She works the whole story of Tereus's unfaithfulness and her own melancholy state into a design in cloth and sends it by an attendant to Progne. Progne reads this fearful message as if it were written in words, rushes frenzied to Philomela's prison, and concealing her sister's face under the foliage of Bacchus as if celebrating his festival, brings her to Tereus's own house. There Progne, pitying the poor woman's overwhelming sorrow, embraces her, but loathing her husband for the crime he has committed, thinks out a scheme of revenge. Shall she burn his palace down and cast him in the flames, or cut out his tongue, as he has cut out her sister's, or shall she stab him to death? While she is thus enraged and thirsting for revenge, Itys, her son, comes into the room. She sees in his face a likeness to his father, and this decides her upon what course she will pursue. While the little fellow's arms are put endearingly about her neck, she drags him to another part of the palace, and, uplifting her sword, strikes him dead. Nor is this enough for revenge: Philomela takes up the sword and cuts his throat, and together the two women mangle his body and put him into a cauldron of boiling water. Then, gloating over her scheme, Progne makes the body into a dish and places it before her husband. Tereus, blind to the nature of the horrible meal, partakes of it, and calls for his little son Itys, that he may also join in the feasting. Then Progne's triumph is complete. She tells her horror-stricken husband that the boy for whom he is asking is the very food that he is eating.

And yet, scarcely understanding, he calls again for Itys; but Philomela, her hair disordered and the marks of the murder upon her, springing forth, throws the head of the boy upon him, and with a loud cry Tereus springs from the table and rushes on the women. With his drawn sword he pursues them into the grounds of the castle, but the gods come to their assistance. While she is making for the woods Philomela is transformed into a nightingale; and Progne, taking refuge beneath the roofs of the buildings, becomes a swallow, upon whose breast even today the red stains of her murdered son appear. Tereus is changed into a crested bird which some versions of the legend say is a hoopoe, others a lapwing:

> "The Thracian king, lamenting sore,
> Turned to a lapwing, doeth them uprayde."

It is from this gruesome fable that the Nightingale is so often called by our poets Philomela or Philomel, and probably the melancholy fate of the king's daughter, whose name the bird bears, is as much responsible for its atmosphere of loneliness and gloom as are its plaintive notes and midnight melody. To mention all the instances in which the nightingale is called by the name of Philomela or Philomel would mean the extension of these pages to an inordinate length. Quite a few must suffice, and these will, at the same time, help to show how the above fable has been influential in associating the bird with grief:

> "Hence with the nightingale will I take part,
> The blessed byrd, that spends her time of sleepe
> In songs and plaintive please the more t'augment
> The memory of hys misdeede that bred her woe."
> -Spenser.

> "Come, Philomel, that sing'st of ravishment.
> Make thy sad grave in my dishevelled hair:
> As the dank earth weeps at thy languishment,
> So I at each sad strain will strain a tear.
> And with deep groans the diapason bear;
> For burden-wise I'll hum on Tarquin still.
> While thou on Tereus descant'st better still."
> -Shakespeare (Lucrece.)

> "Sad Philomel, in bowery shades unseen.
> To vernal airs attunes her varied shades."
> -Pop (Odyssey.)

> "Ah! why, all abandoned to darkness and woe.
> Why, lone Philomela, that languishing fall?"
> -Beattie.

> "And Philomell her song with tears doth steepe."
> -Spenser.

> "King Pandion, he is dead;
> All thy friends are lapp'd in lead;
> All thy fellow-birds do sing.
> Careless of thy sorrowing." -Richard Barnfield.

SUPERSTITIONS ABOUT ANIMALS

"And now and then sweet Philomel would wail."
-Thomson.

"And lonely Philomel still waking sings."
-Matthew Green.

"Less Philomel will deign a song
In her sweetest saddest plight."
-Milton.

"The gentle bird who sings of pity best."
-Charlotte Smith.

"When I departed am, ring thou my knell,
Thou pitiful and pretty Philomel.
-Herrick.

How charming is the Eastern fable that the nightingale is 'in love' with the rose! Picture the sweet little singer in the darkness pouring out its melody to its blushing lady-love from the depths of its tender love-sick heart! This is a favorite theme of the poet Moore:

"The young rose which I gave thee, so dewy and bright.
Was the flow'ret most dear to the sweet bird of night.
Who oft by the moonlight o'er her blushes hath hung,
And thrill'd every leaf with the wild lay he sung.
Oh take thou this young rose, and let her life be
Prolong'd by the breath she will borrow from thee:
For while o'er her bosom thy sweet notes shall trill,
She'll think the sweet night-bird is courting her still."

-The Young Rose.

"Though rich the spot

SUPERSTITIONS ABOUT ANIMALS

With every flow'r this earth has got.
What is it to the nightingale,
If there his darling rose is not?"
-The Light of the Harem.

"And yet, in all that flowery maze
Through which my life has lov'd to tread,
When I have heard the sweetest lays
From lips of dearest lustre shed;
When I have felt the warbled word
From beauty's mouth of perfume sighing.
Sweet as music's hallow'd bird
Upon a rose's bosom lying."
-Poem to Miss Bickford.

"There's a bower of roses by Bendemeer's stream,
And the nightingale sings round it all the day long;
In the time of my childhood 'twas like a sweet dream,
To sit in the roses and hear the bird's song.
That bower and its music I never forget.
But oft when alone in the bloom of the year,
I think- is the nightingale singing there yet?
Are the roses still bright by the calm Bendemeer?"
-Lalla Rookh

Byron, too, sings of the fable:

"For there- the Rose o'er crag or vale,
Sultana of the Nightingale,
The maid for whom his melody,
His thousand songs are heard on high.
Blooms blushing to her lover's tale;
His queen, the garden queen his rose
Unbent by winds, unchill'd by snows.
Far from the winters of the west.

SUPERSTITIONS ABOUT ANIMALS

By every breeze and season blest,
Returns the sweets by nature given
In softest incense back to heaven."
-The Giaour.

"The childish thought was scarcely breathed
Before the rose was pluck'd and wreathed;
The next fond moment saw her seat
Her fairy form at Selim's feet:
'This rose to calm thy brother's cares
A message from the Bulbul (nightingale) bears;
It says to-night it will prolong
For Selim's ear his sweetest song.'"
-The Bride of Abydos.

Lady Mary Wortley Montagu, in her translation of a Turkish love poem, writes:

"The nightingale now wanders in the vines:
Her passion is to seek roses."

Mrs. Browning, in 'A Lay of the Early Rose,' represents the rose as saying:

"Ten nightingales shall flee
Their woods for love of me,
Singing sadly all the suntide,
Never waiting for the moontide."

Probably it is this poetic fable which has given to the nightingale the character of being 'lovelorn,' or it may be derived solely from the plaintiveness of its melody. Whichever it may be, the bird is 'in love.'

"Where the lovelorn nightingale

SUPERSTITIONS ABOUT ANIMALS

Nightly to thee her sad song mourneth well."
-Milton.

"To dear Saint Valentine, no thrush
Sings livelier from a spring-tide bush:
No nightingale her lovelorn tune
More sweetly warbles to the moon."
-Scott.

Shelley, with a touch of realism in his poetry, correctly refers to the enamored songster as the male bird, and describes him pouring out his song to his listening mate. This poet, Byron, and Moore, are among the very few who write of the bird as 'he' nearly all others, probably thinking of poor Philomela, make the songster the female bird. Love, however, is still the nightingale's theme.

"Tis that enamored nightingale
Who gives me the reply;
He ever tells the same soft tale
Of passion and of constancy
To his mate, who rapt and fond
Listening sits, a bough beyond"
-Shelley.

"Hark! that's the nightingale,
Telling the self-same tale
Her song told when this ancient earth was young:
So echoes answered when her song was sung
In the first wooded vale."
-Christina G. Rossetti.

To make 'her' song more pitiful, the bird is represented as perching with its breast pressed against a thorn:

SUPERSTITIONS ABOUT ANIMALS

"Never nightingale so singeth
Oh, she leans on thorny tree.
And her poet soul she flingeth
Over pain to victory."
-E. B. Browning.

"Everything did banish moan.
Save the nightingale alone:
She, poor bird, as all forlorn,
Lean'd her breast up-till a thorn,
And there sung the dolefullest ditty.
That to hear it was great pity."
-Barnfield.

"These nightingales warble the most sweetly.
When they set their breasts against the thorns."
-William Seeker.

"There, as sad Philomel, alike forlorn,
Sings to the night from her accustomed thorn."
-Dr. Darwin.

"No one to soothe me as I sleep
Save Philomel on yonder thorn."
-W.J.Mickle.

"And whiles against a thorn thou bear'st thy part,
To keep thy sharp woes waking, wretched I,
To imitate thee well, against my heart
Will fix a sharp knife to affright mine eye."
-Shakespeare.

Still in the melancholy vein! There is a charming but pathetic fable which is worthy of being inserted here, telling how a nightingale and a shepherd contested for supremacy in the

SUPERSTITIONS ABOUT ANIMALS

richness and variety of song, and how, as the shepherd struck luxurious chords of music from his strings, the sweet bird replied with richer song, until the young musician, breaking forth into 'a full-mouth'd diapason,' the nightingale essayed 'all her sweet powers' to imitate the deep sound, and failing, fell exhausted upon the shepherd's lute and died.

A fine description of this musical contest was written by Richard Crawshaw in the middle of the seventeenth century from the Latin of Strada, and the fable is mentioned at some length about the same period by John Ford, the dramatist, in the Lovers Melancholy, and by several other writers of a later date, Moore and Cowper among the rest. It is not possible or necessary to quote here more than a fragment of Crawshaw's grand poem of a hundred and seventy-five lines, only a few dealing with the pathetic finish of the contest must suffice:

> "At length (after so long, so loud a strife
> Of all the strings, still -breathing the best life
> Of blest variety, attending on
> His fingers' fairest revolution,
> In many a sweet rise, many as sweet a fall
> A full-mouth'd diapason swallows all.
> This done, he lists what she would say to this;
> And she, although her breath's late exercise
> Had dealt too roughly with her tender throat,
> Yet summons all her sweet powers for a note.
> Alas! in vain! for while (sweet soul) she tries
> To measure all those wild diversities
> Of chatt'ring strings, by the small size of one
> Poor simple voice, raised in a natural tone;
> She fails, and failing grieves, and grieving dies:
> She dies, and leaves her life the victor's prize.
> Falling upon his lute; oh fit to have
> (That lived so sweetly) dead, so sweet a grave."

SUPERSTITIONS ABOUT ANIMALS

John Ford's description, given in dialogue, is neither so full nor so rich as Crawshaw's, but he has embodied the pathos of the scene, and has given us the phrase: "A nightingale. Nature's best skill'd musician," which choicely expresses an almost universal opinion.

The following is an extract from the Lovers' Melancholy. Menaphon is describing to Amethus the contest he has seen in a grove at Thessaly:

"The young man grew at last
Into a pretty anger, that a bird
Whom art had never taught clefs, moods, or notes,
Should vie with him for mastery, whose study
Had busied many hours to perfect practice;
To end the controversy, in a rapture
Upon his instrument he plays so swiftly,
So many voluntaries, and so quick.
That there was curiosity and cunning,
Concord in discord, lines of differing method
Meeting in one full center of delight.
The bird, ordain'd to be
Music's first martyr, strove to imitate
These several sounds: which, when her warbling throat
Fail'd in, for grief, down dropp'd she on his lute,
And brake her heart !"

Moore's reference to the fable is contained in a few lines describing Zelica's sad melody when she sings to the obligate of her lute:

"And when she sung to her lute's touching strain
'Twas like the notes, half ecstasy, half pain,
The bulbul utters, ere her soul depart,
When, vanquish'd by some minstrel's powerful art.

SUPERSTITIONS ABOUT ANIMALS

She dies upon the lute whose sweetness broke her heart."

Cowper deals with the fable in a poem of four verses, which he calls 'Strada's Nightingale':

"The shepherd touch'd his reed; sweet Philomel
Essay'd, and oft essay'd to catch the strain,
And treasuring, as on her ear they fell,
The numbers, echo'd note for note again.
The peevish youth, who ne'er had found before
A rival of his skill, indignant heard.
And soon (for various was his tuneful store)
In loftier tones defied the simple bird.
She dared the task, and rising as he rose
With all the force that passion gives inspired,
Return'd the sound awhile, but in the close
Exhausted fell, and at his feet expired.
Thus strength, not skill prevail'd. O fatal strife.
By thee, poor songstress, playfully begun;
And, O sad victory, which cost thy life.
And he may wish that he had never won."

Is it anything more than a mere coincidence that one of the notes of the nightingale is 'tereu,' while the name of the king who dealt so wickedly with poor Philomela in the fable was Tereus? Is it not quite probable that the name of the king was suggested by the note of the bird? Richard Barnfield seems to suggest this in one of his sonnets, from which I have previously quoted:

"'Fie, fie, fie,' now would she cry;
'Tereu, tereu' by-and-by;
That to hear her so complain.
Scarce I could from tears refrain."

And later in the same sonnet he mentions the name of King Pandion, the father of Philomela, who being dead cannot pity her. John Lyly, the dramatist, also mentions this note in the bird's song as if it had something to do with 'her woes';

"What bird so sings, yet so does wail.
O, 'tis the ravish'd nightingale.
Jug, jug, jug, jug, tereu- she cries,
And still her woes at midnight rises."

As we have noticed when giving the first two quotations of the nightingale, the bird is supposed to be singing of Tereus, who, as Spenser puts it, "bred her woe"; and Lord Thurlow is another poet who uses the name in the same connection:

"When with the jacinth
Coy fountains are tressed ;
And for the mournful bird
Greenwoods are dressed.
That did for Tereus pine;
Then shall our songs be thine,
To whom our hearts incline:
May, be thou blessed!"

A very poetic, but quite erroneous, supposition is that a Pelican feeds her young with blood which she draws from her own breast. Keats tells us that;

"Life's self is nourished by its proper pith.
And we are nurtured like a pelican brood."

Byron goes so far as to give a picture of the pelican destroying her own life to feed her nestlings;

"It is as if the desert bird

SUPERSTITIONS ABOUT ANIMALS

Whose beak unlocks her bosom's stream
To still her famished nestlings' scream,
Nor mourns a life to them transferr'd,
Should rend her rash devoted breast,
And find them flown her empty nest."

Moore even more definitely declares:

"No, thy chains as they rankle, thy blood as it runs.
But make thee more painfully dear to thy sons,
Whose hearts, like the young of the desert-bird's nest,
Drink love in each life-drop that flows from thy breast."

So perfect a picture of maternal love and solicitude is this poetic fable, that one is truly sorry to deny that it has any foundation in truth. The horribly plain and unromantic foundation of the belief is that the pelican, when feeding her voracious young, presses her bill against her breast to disgorge the fish contained in her capacious pouch. The fact of the tip of the bird's bill being red has been quite enough to create the touching story that the pelican gives of her own life's blood to nourish her tender offspring. The story that Swans sing a sweet song 'tinged with pathos' before they die is of very ancient origin. Ovid was familiar with the fable, and makes use of it to describe poor Canens' lamentation for her woodpecker husband:

"Six nights and as many returning lights of the sun beheld her, destitute of sleep and of food, going over hills and valleys, wherever chance led her. Tiber, last of all, beheld her worn out with weeping, and wandering, and reposing her body on his cold banks. There, with tears, she poured forth words attuned, lamenting, in a low voice, her very woes, as when the swan, now about to die, sings his own funeral dirge. At last, melting with grief, even to her thin marrow, she pined away, and by degrees vanished into light. And in the same translation

SUPERSTITIONS ABOUT ANIMALS

(Riley's) the poet also writes:

"The white swan, as he lies on the wet grass when the Fates summon him, sings at the fords of Maender."

The theme has been a favourite one with the poets:

"I will play the song and die in music."
-Shakespeare (Othello.)

"And now this pale swan in her watery nest
Begins the sad dirge of her certain ending."
-Shakespeare (Lucrece)

"Then, if he lose, he makes a swan-like end.
Fading in music."
-Shakespeare (Merchant of Venice)

"And over the pond are sailing
Two swans all white as snow;
Sweet voices mysteriously wailing
Pierce through me as onward they go.
They sail along, and a ringing
Sweet melody rises on high,
And when the swans begin singing
They presently must die."
-Heine.

"There swan-like let me sing and die."
-Byron.

"A dying swan of Pindus sings
In mildly mournful strains."
-Robert Montgomery.

SUPERSTITIONS ABOUT ANIMALS

"Like some full-breasted swan
That, fluting a wild carol ere her death,
Ruffles her pure cold plume and takes the flood
With swarthy webs."
-Tennyson (The Passing of Arthur)

"With an inner voice the river ran,
Adown it floated a dyipg swan,
And loudly did lament."
-Tennyson (The Dying Swan)

"Swans sing before they die: 'twere no bad thing
Should certain persons die before they sing."
-Coleridge.

Many other poets have also made similar references to the same fable, and from Whittier's 'Swan Song of Parson Avery,' in which the poet says that "The soul of Father Avery went singing to his rest," we may gather that this old idea is one of several that have found their way across the Atlantic, others being the British legend of the Robin and the custom of 'Telling the Bees.' There is no more beautiful or poetic story than how the Crossbill derived its name. The legend can best be told in Longfellow's sympathetic poem:

"On the cross the dying Saviour
Heavenward lifts His eyelids calm,
Feels, but scarcely feels, a trembling
In His pierced and bleeding palm.
And by all the world forsaken,
Sees He how with zealous care
At the ruthless nails of iron
A little bird is striving there.
Stained with blood and never tiring
With its beak it doth not cease.

SUPERSTITIONS ABOUT ANIMALS

From the cross 'twould free the Saviour,
Its Creator's Son release.
And the Saviour speaks in mildness:
'Blest be thou of all the good!
Bear, as token of this moment,
Marks of blood and holy rood!
And that bird is called the crossbill;
Covered all with blood so clear.
In the groves of pine it singeth
Songs, like legends, strange to hear."

A fable of a different kind, yet not far behind the legend of the crossbill in beauty and poetic feeling, is that of the Peacock's hatred of gold. So intense is its dislike of this much prized metal that it will not alight on ground where it may be found. Major Campbell writes of this fable in an interesting and neatly worded poem:

"The peacock with its plumage rare
Is a holy bird and wise;
For he knows that gold is an evil thing.
From which foul thoughts and fancies spring,
To blind our mortal eyes;
He knows It is the seed of sin
Whose fruit may ripen the soul within;
For (if legends tell true) he will not tread
On the earth of the track that covers its bed."

Why the peacock, of all birds, should be singled out to assume the rôle of a mammon-hater we are not told, nor is it easy to discover. From his gaudy plumage and proud demeanor, one would hardly suppose that he had so strong an antipathy to gold or ornament of any sort. A very quaint and weird superstition, which was common in the days when sprites and pixies were supposed to hold midnight revels, and, for good or

SUPERSTITIONS ABOUT ANIMALS

ill, pay visits to mortals in whom they were interested, was that at the first crow of the Cock at early morn the spirits which had been at liberty since midnight, goblins, pixies, fairies, and all immortals, betook themselves to their own abodes.

> "Now it's the time of night
> That the graves all gaping wide,
> Every one lets forth his sprite,
> In the church-way paths to glide."

There are many references to this old superstition in our literature, quite the best of which is in the opening scene of Hamlet, where, on the castle platform, we find Bernardo, Horatio, and Marcellus discussing the subject after the precipitate disappearance of the melancholy ghost of Hamlet's murdered father.

> "Bernardo. It was about to speak when the cock crew.
> Horatio. And then it started, like a guilty thing
> Upon a fearful summons. I have heard
> The cock, that is trumpet to the morn,
> Doth with his lofty and shrill sounding throat
> Awake the god of day: and at his warning,
> Whether in sea or fire, in earth or air,
> The extravagant and erring spirit hies
> To his confine: and the truth herein
> This present object made probation.
> Marcellus. It faded on the crowing of the cock."

This barn-door signal for the return of spirits and fairies to their own quarters is mentioned by Milton in his poem 'L'Allegro.' In this instance the immortal concerned is a 'goblin,' and the poet introduces the quaint custom of leaving a bowl of milk for the goblin to drink as a reward for his midnight labors. We read:

SUPERSTITIONS ABOUT ANIMALS

"How the drudging goblin sweat
To earn his cream-bowl duly set,
When in one night, ere glimpse of morn,
His shadowy flail hath thresh'd the corn,
That ten day-labourers could not end;
Then lies him down the lubber fiend,
And stretch'd out all the chimney's length,
Basks at the fire his hairy strength;
And crop-full out of doors he flings
Ere thefirst cock his matin rings."

David Mallet, or Mallock, the Scotch poet, refers to the superstition in his poem "William and Margaret":

"Twas at the silent solemn hour
When night and morning meet;
In glided Margaret's grimly ghost
And stood at William's feet."

Then Margaret proceeds to reproach her lover in his unfaithfulness, which has caused her death:

"'Awake!' she cried, 'thy true love calls.
Come from her midnight grave:
Now let thy pity hear the maid
Thy love refused to save.
This is the dark and dreary hour
When injured ghosts complain;
When yawning graves give up their dead
To haunt the faithless swain.'"

But while she still upbraids her trembling William the cock crows:

"But hark! the cock has warned me hence;

SUPERSTITIONS ABOUT ANIMALS

A long and last adieu!
Come see, false man, how low she lies
Who died for love of you.'"

In his poem, 'Mary's Dream,' John Lowe describes a similar incident. In this case, however, the ghost is a male, the sailor-love of Sweet Mary, who dreams 'of Sandy far at sea.' Sandy comes to her bedside and tells her that he has perished, but:

"The storm is past and I at rest;
So Mary weep no more for me!"

But while the ghost is speaking comfort to the girl,

"Loud crowed the cock, the shadow fled,
No more of Sandy could she see;
But soft the passing spirit said,
'Sweet Mary, weep no more for me.'"

Herrick has a passage in one of his 'Hesperides,' in which the cock recalls his mistress while she is inviting him to Elizium:

"But harke, I heare the Cock,
(The bellman of the night) proclaim the clock
Of late struck one; and now I see the prime
Of day break from the pregnant East, 'tis time
I vanish; more I had to say;
But night determines here, Away."

Ben Jonson, in his Masque of Queens, gives the cock-crow as the signal for witches to cease from their loathsome practices:

"I last night lay all alone

SUPERSTITIONS ABOUT ANIMALS

On the ground to hear the mandrake groan;
And plucked him up though he grew full low;
And as I had done the cock did crow."

In the scene from Hamlet which I have quoted,
Marcellus goes on to relate a pretty fable which, however poetic
it may be, I am glad to say for the comfort of our slumbers is
easily proved untrue- that at Christmas-time the cock does not
cease to crow throughout the night, so that spirits may not
desecrate the season of our Savior's birth:

"Marcellus. Some say, that ever 'gainst that season
comes
Wherein our Saviour's birth is celebrated.
The bird of dawning singeth all night long:
And then, they say, no spirit dare stir abroad;
The nights are wholesome; then no planets strike.
No fairy takes, nor witch hath power to charm.
So hallow'd and so gracious is the time."

Tennyson, in his 'Morte d'Arthur,' has a reference
to this poetic fable:

"The cock crew loud: as at that time of year
The lusty bird takes every hour for dawn.
I awoke, and heard indeed
The clear church bells ring in the Christmas morn."

How often we hear the words 'Halcyon Days' spoken of
without thinking, or perhaps caring to know, how they entered
into our common phraseology. We know the meaning which they
convey- days of tranquility; or, as the dictionary tells us, 'days of
quiet prosperity.' But Halcyon Days are more than a mere current
phrase, they are a link which unites us with a very ancient
superstition. The halcyon of the ancients was the Kingfisher, that

beautiful, but now unfortunately rare, bird, which the gun of the collector seems likely to make altogether extinct; and it was the poetical notion of these people that the kingfishers possessed the power of keeping the water calm while they built their nests upon its surface. The days during which the water was said to remain quiescent were the seven days before the winter solstice and the seven days after, and were known as Halcyon Days- days during which the water remained calm. The ancient fable associated with the name of these resplendent birds is replete with a tender charm and pathos which is worth mentioning in the interest of those who have not heard it.

Ceyx the King of Trachyn, being disturbed in his mind respecting the fate of his brother, determines on consulting the oracle at Claros, and makes known his intention to his wife, Halcyone. She pleads with tears that he will take her with him and let her share by his side the dangers of the long and hazardous voyage; but Ceyx cannot think of his beloved Halcyone being placed in such a direful position, and he gently refuses her request. Then Halcyone seeing that her request will not be granted, and feeling a presentiment of the fate which is to overtake her husband, falls at his feet in a swoon. When she raises her weeping eyes the ship is on the seas and Ceyx is waving his hand to her in farewell; and, watching it till the sails disappear from view, Halcyone returns to her home and weeps for her beloved husband. True to the presentiment of Halcyone, a great storm overtakes the ship on which Ceyx is journeying to Claros, and, unable to battle with the waves, it sinks to the bottom of the ocean. Ceyx, with a few of the sailors who do not go down with the sunken vessel, clings to a spar and for a while keeps upon the surface of the water; but presently a great dark billow overwhelms him, and he is engulfed. All this while, faithful Halcyone is praying for the safety of her husband, and making every preparation for his return before the end of two months, as he had promised. But the fate of her husband is made known to her. Morpheus flies through the dark to her bedside, and taking upon him the form of the ill-fated Ceyx, tells her that the prayers she has offered in his behalf have availed him nothing, for he has perished on his voyage. Halcyone, on hearing this dire news, is overcome with anguish. She wildly beats her face and breast, and rushing to the sea-shore, where she had last seen her husband when he set sail to Claros, she declares that she cannot live without him, and resolves to go to him in the sea. But while she is standing by the side of the sea, she sees a body floating upon the water, and, as she watches it, the waves bring it nearer and nearer to her. Then she recognizes in this body the form of her unfortunate husband, and she springs upon a mole in the sea to clasp him. But, even as she leaps upon the stones, wings bear her upon the surface of the water, and she becomes transformed into a kingfisher. With her bill she kisses the dead face of her beloved Ceyx; with her wings she embraces him, and the gods having compassion upon her, change her husband also into a kingfisher so that as birds their love might remain unchanged. And thereafter, when they rested upon the face of the waters, the sea remained calm, and "the passage of the deep was safe."

As might be supposed, so beautiful and tender a story has commended itself to the fancy of the poets. Very few of the many references to the fable must suffice:

"O magic sleep! O comfortable bird
That broodest o'er the troubled sea of mind
Till it is hush'd and smooth."
-Keats.

"And close beside her lay a delicate fan.
Made of the halcyon's blue wing; and when
She looked upon it, it would calm her thoughts
As that bird calms the ocean." -Longfellow.

SUPERSTITIONS ABOUT ANIMALS

"And, over all, the blessed sun,
Telling of halcyon days begun."
-D. M. Moir.

"The weary there lay down to rest.
And there the halcyon built her nest."
-James Montgomery.

"While birds of calm sit brooding on the charmed
waves."
-Milton.

"So shall the Church, thy bright and mystic bride.
Sit on the stormy gulf a halcyon bird of calm."
-H. H. Milman.

"Far, far away, O ye
Halcyons of memory.
Seek some far calmer nest
Than this abandoned breast.'"
-Shelley.

So long as this last-named poet dealt with the halcyon as
a symbol of tranquility he was safe, but when he overstepped this
limit and introduced natural history into his poetry, he at once
fell into a great error. Had he watched 'two azure halcyons'
procuring their food, he would not have ventured to write:

"I cannot tell my joy, when, o'er a lake
Upon a drooping bough with night-shade twined,
I saw two azure halcyons clinging downward
And thinning one bright bunch of amber berries.
With quick long beaks, and on the deep there lay
Those lovely forms imaged as in a sky."

SUPERSTITIONS ABOUT ANIMALS

"Amber berries" are a very strange diet for fish-eating birds! Figuier, the celebrated naturalist, tells us that to the dead body of the kingfisher "the attributes of turning aside thunderbolts, of giving beauty, peace, and plenty, and other absurdities were ascribed. Even now, in some remote provinces in France, the dead birds are invested with the power of preserving woolen stuffs from the attacks of moths; hence they are called moth-birds by drapers and shopkeepers."

Another faculty which the dead body of the kingfisher is said to possess is that of pointing its bill in the direction from which wind may be expected. There seems to be a reference to this quaint superstition in Dryden's 'Hind and Panther,' although no mention is made of the bird itself:

"High on the oak, which never leaf shall bear,
He breathed his last, exposed to open air;
And there his corpse unblessed is hanging still,
To show the change of winds with his prophetic bill."

Dryden is here writing of the martin, but that the 'prophetic bill' has reference to the superstition mentioned above seems certain, for there is no such belief associated with the martin. Of that social, pugnacious little bird the Robin Redbreast,

"Sweetest of all the feathered throng," many pretty fables are told, and there are no stories about any of our birds more charming than how the robin's breast became red. In England there are two of these legends, both of which have their foundations in an act of charity, one to our Savior, and the other to poor tormented souls in hell. The first of these legends is that when the Savior hung in agony upon the Cross a sympathetic robin, then a plain, unattractive little bird, pitied His sufferings and wrested the thorns from the crown which tore His brow. In performing this act of charity the blood from the thorn-marks

SUPERSTITIONS ABOUT ANIMALS

dyed the bird's breast red, in memory of which the feathers have ever since retained this color. The American writer, Delle Whitney Norton, has put this legend into poetry:

> "On fair Britannia's isle, bright bird,
> A legend strange is told of thee
> 'Tis said thy blithesome song was hushed
> While Christ toiled up Mount Calvary,
> Bowed 'neath the sins of all mankind;
> And humbled to the very dust
> By the vile cross, while viler man
> Mocked with a crown of thorns the Just.
> Pierced by our sorrows, and weighed down
> By our transgressions,- faint and weak.
> Crushed by an angry judge's frown,
> And agonies no word can speak,-
> 'Twas then, dear bird, the legend says.
> That thou from out His crown, didst tear
> The thorns, to lighten the distress.
> And ease the pain that He must bear,
> While pendent from thy tiny beak
> The gory points thy bosom pressed.
> And crimsoned with thy Saviour's blood
> The sober brownness of thy breast!
> Since which proud hour for thee and thine,
> As an especial sign of grace
> God pours like sacramental wine
> Red signs of favor o'er thy race!"

The other story is best told in the words of Whittier:

> "My old Welsh neighbour, over the way
> Crept slowly out in the sun of Spring,
> Pushed from her ears the locks of gray,
> And listened to hear the robins sing.

SUPERSTITIONS ABOUT ANIMALS

Her grandson, playing at marbles, stopped,
And, cruel in sport as boys will be.
Tossed a stone at the bird, who hopped
From bough to bough in the apple-tree.
'Nay!' said the grandmother, ' have you not heard,
My poor, bad boy! of the fiery pit,
And how, drop by drop, this merciful bird
Carries the water that quenches it?
'He brings cool dew in his little bill,
And lets it fall on the souls of sin;
You can see the marks on his red bireast still
Of fires that scorch as he drops it in.
'My poor Bron rhuddyn! my breast-burned bird.
Singing so sweetly from limb to limb.
Very dear to the heart of our Lord
Is he who pities the lost like Him.'"

In another poem by the same sweet singer of New
England, we are told how the Algonquin Indians account for the
redness of the robin's breast. This legend is really too romantic to
omit, although, according to my first intention, it should not have
a place here:

"Once a great chief left his son,-
Well-beloved, his only one,-
When the boy was well-nigh grown.
In the trial lodge alone.
Left for tortures long and slow
Youths like him must undergo
Who their pride of manhood test,
Lacking water, food, and rest."

And here seven days and seven nights he was kept until-

"Wrung with pain. Weak from nature's overstrain," he

moaned; "Spare me, father, for I faint!" But "the chieftain, haughty eyed," was obdurate, wishing to see his son a great warrior, and so replying:

> "Better you should starving die
> Than that boy and squaw should cry
> Shame upon your father's son,"

He left the youth again in the trial lodge alone. But... "When next morn the sun's first rays- Glistened on the hemlock sprays," the chief went to the lodge with food for his brave lad, he 'found the poor boy dead.' And as they dug a grave for him they saw upon the lodge-top overhead a bird they had never seen before, "Preening smooth its breast of red," and the bird told them never more to mourn for him, because, it said: "I, a bird, am still your son."

Then it told them how as a:

> "Friend of man, my song shall cheer
> Lodge and corn land; hovering near
> To each wigwam, I shall bring
> Tidings of the coming spring.'
> Thus the Indian legend saith
> How, at first the robin came
> With a sweeter life from death
> Bird for boy and still the same."

Wordsworth, it would seem, had in his mind the beautiful English legends of the robin-redbreast when he wrote:

> "Art thou the bird whom man loves best.
> The pious bird with the scarlet breast.
> Our little English robin?"

SUPERSTITIONS ABOUT ANIMALS

And Thomson, similarly, writes of the redbreast as "Sacred to the household gods." But there are, perhaps, very few of us who think of these legends, or have even heard of them, when we give our warmest affection to this saucy, sociable bird. It is for some other reason that the redbreast is universally loved, and that it has been chosen as an emblem of piety. Probably its trustful, sociable nature has awakened a responsive chord in our own hearts, for are we not generally touched by an appeal to our purest and truest instincts? Other birds are equally pretty and melodious, but none is so dear to us as the robin:

> "The bird, whom by some name or other,
> All men who know thee call thee brother.
> The darling of children and men."

How touched were our impressionable little hearts in our baby days when we listened to the woeful tale of the robin's death and his melancholy interment. How cordially we detested the sparrow, plain, chirruping plebeian, for letting his cruel arrow penetrate the red breast of our poor pet bird; and we felt a thrill of tender pity when we were told that:

> "All the birds of the air
> Fell a-sighing and a-sobbing
> When they heard of the death
> Of poor cock robin."

It seemed quite natural that the robin should be chosen from all other birds to perform the pious act of covering the poor Babes in the Wood with leaves; indeed, the robin is the very bird we ourselves would have chosen had we written the story. Imagine the giddy tomtit, or the stately wagtail, or the portly bullfinch, though he too has a red breast, or the gaudy goldfinch covering the little wanderers with a funeral pall of leaves and flowers! No, only the robin would do. So it is to the robin-redbreast Herrick appeals for the same kindly office when he dies:

> "Laid out for dead, let thy last kindnesse be
> With leaves and mosse-work for to cover me :
> And while the Wood-nymphs my cold corps inter,
> Sing thou my Dirge, sweet warbling Chorister!
>
> For Epitaph, in Foliage, next write this,
> Here, here, the tomb of Robin Herrick is."

It is surprising how many of our poets have left us a memorial of this pretty fable. In addition to the above, three others must suffice:

> "Their little corpse the robin redbreasts found.
> And strewed with pious bill the leaves around."
> -Gav.
>
> "Call for the robin-redbreast and the wren,
> Since o'er shady groves they hover.
> And with leaves and flowers do cover
> The friendless bodies of unburied men."
> -John Webster.
>
> "The redbreast oft at evening hours
> Shall kindly lend his little aid.
> With hoary moss, and gathered flowers.
> To deck the ground were thou art laid."
> -William Collins.

Webster's association of the Wren with the redbreast in covering 'the bodies of unburied men' reminds us of the common supposition that Jenny Wren, as the bird is called, and Cock Robin are linked together as husband and wife:

SUPERSTITIONS ABOUT ANIMALS

"The robin and the wren
Are God Almighty's cock and hen."

Who has ever heard of a hen robin or a cock wren? But, unfortunately, poor Jenny Wren has no pretty fables to make her 'pious,' nor is she permitted to rank so high in the opinion of mankind as her 'husband,' "The darling of children and men."

Indeed, all the fables told about her- or had we not better say him? since he is a king- are very much the reverse of complimentary. He is supposed to be an emissary of the devil, and to have obtained his ancient title of 'King of all Birds' by perpetrating a fraud. As we are told in Grimm's story of 'King Wren':

"In a grand assembly of all the birds of the air, it was determined that the sovereignty of the feathered tribe should be conferred upon the one who would fly highest. The favorite was, of course, the eagle, who at once, and in full confidence of victory, commenced his flight towards the sun; when he had vastly distanced all competitors, he proclaimed with a mighty voice his victory over all things that had wings. Suddenly, however, the wren, who had secreted himself under the feathers of the eagle's crest, popped from his hiding-place, flew a few inches upwards, and chirped out as loudly as he could, 'Birds, look up and behold your king'; and was elected accordingly.'"

This fraudulently obtained title of 'King of all Birds' is of very antique origin. Tradition dates it as far back as the days of the Druids, and the Manx name for the bird, Dreain, is derived from the two words druai dryw, the Druid's bird. The name of the wren in several European languages upholds this kingly title, and at the same time shows that the source of it must be at least as ancient as tradition makes it. For example, the Latin name of the bird is Regulus; the French, Roitelet; Welsh, Bren (king);

SUPERSTITIONS ABOUT ANIMALS

Teutonic, Konig Vogel (king bird); Dutch, Konije (little king). While referring to this subject in his Collectanea de Rebus Hibernicis, Colonel Vallency says:

"The Druids represented this as the king of all birds. The superstitious respect shown to this little bird gave offense to our first Christian missionaries, and by their commands he is still hunted and killed by the peasants on Christmas Day, and on the following (St. Stephen's Day) he is carried about hung by the leg in the center of two hoops crossing each other at right angles, and a procession made in every village of men, women, and children, singing an Irish catch, reporting him to be the king of all birds."

One of the verses of this 'catch' to which the writer refers is as follows:

"The wren, the wren, the king of all birds,
We have caught, St, Stephen's Day, in the furze;
Although he is little, his family's great,
I pray you, good dame, do give us a treat."

The hunting of the wren here alluded to on St. Stephen's Day, or during Christmas week, was formerly common in Ireland, the Isle of Man, some counties in England, and in certain parts of the Continent; nor is the old custom even yet altogether obsolete, though it is mainly confined to the senseless massacre of the birds by schoolboys. Another reason for the hunting of the wren is given by Aubrey in his Miscellanies. He says that after a battle in Ireland, "a party of the Protestants had been surprised sleeping by the Popish Irish, were it not for several wrens that just wakened them by dancing and pecking on the drums as the enemy were approaching. For this reason the wild Irish mortally hate these birds to this day, calling them the devil's servants, and killing them wherever they can catch them; they teach their children to thrust them full of thorns; you'll see sometimes on holidays a whole parish running like madmen from hedge to hedge a wren hunting."

Whatever may have been the origin of this quaint but cruel custom, it spread so quickly that two centuries ago the inhabitants of villages far enough remote from Ireland to be uninterested in the squabbles between Romanists and Protestants turned the hunting of the wren into an annual festival. The custom as it was carried out in the Isle of Man until comparatively recent days is well described by George Waldron in his Description of the Isle of Man. The following extract from this work appears in the Mona Miscellany., vol. xvi., for the use of which I am much indebted to Mr. Thomas Cowley, Ramsey, Isle of Man. The period of which Mr. Waldron writes was about two centuries ago. He says:

"On the 24th of December, towards evening, all the servants in general have a holiday; they go not to bed all night, but ramble about till the bells ring in all the churches, which is at twelve o'clock; prayers being over, they go to hunt the wren, and after having found one of these poor birds, they kill her, and lay her on a bier with the utmost solemnity, bringing her to the parish church, and burying her with a whimsical kind of solemnity, singing dirges over her in the Manx language, which they call her knell, after which Christmas begins."

Commenting on this, the editor of the Miscellany, William Harrison, says: "This custom of 'Hunting the Wren' has been a pastime in the Isle of Man from time immemorial, and is still (1869) kept up on St Stephen's Day, chiefly by boys, who at early dawn sally out armed with long sticks, beating the bushes until they find one of these birds, when they commence the chase with great shoutings, following it from bush to bush, and when killed it is suspended in a garland of ribbons, flowers, and evergreens. The procession then commences, carrying that 'King of all the Birds,' as the Druids called it, from house to house, soliciting contributions, and giving a feather for luck; these are considered an effectual preservative from shipwreck, and some fishermen will not yet venture out to sea without having first provided themselves with a few of these feathers to ensure their safe return. The drein, or wren's feathers, are considered an effectual preservative against witchcraft. It was formerly the custom in the evening to inter the naked body with great solemnity in a secluded corner of the churchyard, and conclude the evening with wrestling and all manner of sports.

The custom is not peculiar to the Isle of Man, for we find it mentioned by Sonnini in his travels, that 'the inhabitants of the town of Cistat, near Marseilles, armed with sabers and pistols, commence the anniversary by hunting the wren, and when captured is suspended, as though it were a heavy burden, from the middle of a long pole borne on the shoulders of two men, carried in procession through the streets, and weighed on a balance.'

Crofton Croker, in his Researches in the South of Ireland, 1824, mentions this custom as prevailing there, and in Hall's Ireland it is also recorded, to which is added the air to the song as penned by Mr. Alexander D. Roche, as also a spirited woodcut of the wren-boys with their garland. The air is also given in Barrow's Mona Melodies, 1820."

There are various versions of this song; one of these, taken down by Mr. Harrison from a company of 'wren-boys' in 1843, is a curious piece of composition. Beginning with the party going to the woods in search of a wren, the story is sung of its capture, death, and final consumption. The Manx air to which the song is sung is a spirited and 'catchy' melody, and has deservedly become popular in the island. One verse of the song must suffice as an example of all the others:

> "We'll away to the woods, says Robin to Bobbin;
> We'll away to the woods, says Richard to Robin;
> We'll away to the woods, says Jack of the Land;
> We'll away to the woods, says every one."

The next verse consists of the line:

"What shall we do there, says Robin to Bobbin," repeated as above, and following this comes another line treated in the same way: "We will hunt the wren, says Robin to Bobbin," and so on all through the song. A curious feature of 'Hunt the Wren,' and one to which the editor of the Miscellany calls attention, is "that wherever we find this peculiar custom prevailing, it is always attended with appliances, as if the object sought for was one of extraordinary bulk or weight, instead of being one of the most diminutive of our feathered tribe."

Thus we have the lines:

"How shall we get him home? says Robin to Bobbin," and the reply in the next verse is: "We'll hire a cart, says Robin to Bobbin."

Following verses tell how the pygmy bird is boiled "in the brewery pan," placed therein with "iron bars and a rope," taken out with "a long pitchfork," and eaten with "knives and forks."

In Sonnini's description of the custom in France he tells us that the wren was hunted with "sabers and pistols," and when captured was "suspended, as though it were a heavy burden, from the middle of a long pole borne on the shoulders of two men.", "The origin of this," says Mr. Harrison, "is not mentioned

by any writer that I have consulted; it may, perhaps, be
accounted for by the desire to render every homage to so
important a personage as 'the king of all birds,' Who, like other
potentates, requires every appliance that can be devised to
uphold and maintain his dignity; whatever the origin, however, it
is certain that it has continued from the earliest ages. The old
tune of 'Hoist, hoist,' is said to come from the Anglo-Saxon
times, and is the burden of the song as sung in Devonshire in
Christmas week, where the villagers formerly suspended the
wren from a heavy pole and carried on their shoulders as a
mighty burden. They pretended to hoist the monstrous bird into a
wagon, singing as follows:

> 'I've shot a wren', says Robin to Bobbin;
> Hoist! hoist! says Richard to Robin;
> Hoist! hoist! says John all alone;
> Hoist! hoist! says every one,'

...and so on, always chorusing with affected labor
and exertion, 'Hoist! Hoist!'"

Happily for the preservation of this pretty, restless little
bird, the stupid and wicked custom of hunting it at Christmas-
tide is almost extinct, and will, I hope, soon be entirely so. In
whatever way the custom originated, nothing good could come
of it. Quite the reverse, it fostered a spirit of wanton destruction,
which, unfortunately, is already too prominent a characteristic of
the average boy, and it was a gross injustice to the smallest and
least harmful of all our feathered friends. In England, I am glad
to say, the custom never obtained any very great vogue. To most
people little Jenny Wren has always been a bird to be protected,
'an unlucky bird to kill;' even to desecrate their nests would bring
misfortune to the rash destroyer, for, as I have said elsewhere:

"The robin and the wren,

SUPERSTITIONS ABOUT ANIMALS

Are God Almighty's cock and hen."

"Him that harries their nest.
Never shall his soul have rest;"

or, as an old poet renders the same adage:

"I never take away their nest, nor try
To catch the old ones, lest a friend should die;
Dick took a wren's nest from his cottage side.
And ere a twelvemonth past his mother dy'd."

That prettily-colored and sweet-voiced bird the Yellowhammer is another of our feathered friends who unjustly suffer at the hands of thoughtless people.

"Fair plumaged bird! cursed by the causeless hate
Of every schoolboy."

Youngsters seem to think they are doing a proper and natural thing in wounding the bird or ruthlessly tearing its nest to pieces; and this dislike, sad to say, in country districts is shared by older people who should have more sense with the increase of years. Most probably the persecution of this pretty and gentle bird has arisen from a stupid old legend which says that on the first day of May the Devil inoculates the yellowhammer with three drops of his own blood. But how many of the boys or men who persecute the yellowhammer can give any reason why they do so? They are prejudiced against it, but they little know that their prejudice has arisen from so stupid and wicked a belief!

From our earliest days we have been ready to accept any strange stories about Ostriches which our school-books and 'popular' works of natural history have been pleased to tell us. We have been led to believe that these birds are 'Silliest of the feathered kind,' and when we have turned to our Bibles and read that 'God hath deprived her of wisdom, neither hath he imparted to her understanding,' we have considered the matter quite settled. But we shall do well not to arrive too hastily at any such conclusion. The ostrich is a bird which has been very much misunderstood. Its character and habits were described long before they were sufficiently investigated, and all sorts of silly stories were circulated about it, most of which had only a slight foundation of truth. Now that the birds are reared on farms by the thousands, very much after the manner of tame poultry, and there has been ample opportunity to study their habits and nature, the exaggerated yarns of an earlier day are being accepted at their proper worth. In some respects the ostrich displays a remarkable lack of intelligence, but the popular yarn that it hides its head in sand when pursued, under the fond delusion that because it cannot see its pursuers therefore they cannot see the bird itself, is utterly void of truth. When Moore tells us that:

> "Whole nations, fooled by falsehood, fear, or pride.
> Their ostrich heads in self-illusion hide,"

...he merely repeats a common fallacy, and, as a poet, is ready to introduce a serviceable illustration, for which he may be excused; but it is significant that in the book of Job, where the character of the ostrich is sketched to some length, no mention is made of this supposed gross stupidity. The bird's habit of burying her eggs in sand and leaving them to hatch by the heat of the sun is mentioned in several verses:

> "Gavest thou the goodly wings unto the peacocks? or
> wings and feathers unto the ostrich?
> Which leaveth her eggs in the earth, and warmeth them
> in dust,
> And forgetteth that the foot may crush them, or that the

wild beast may break them.
She is hardened against her young ones, as though they were not hers: her labor is in vain without fear."

In Lamentations there is also a reference to this habit:

"Even the sea-monsters draw out the breast, they give suck to their young ones: the daughter of my people is become cruel, like the ostriches in the wilderness."

The poets, too, have caught hold of this want of maternal instinct:

"Hast thou expelled the mother from thy breast.
And to the desert's mercies left thy nest?"

...asks Montgomery, and the bird answers:

"Ah! no; the mother in me knows her part,
Yon glorious sun is warmer than my heart."

But Cowper, giving the bird no opportunity of speaking for herself, declares:

"The ostrich, silliest of the feathered kind.
And formed of God without a parent's mind,
Commits her eggs, uncautious, to the dust."

Montgomery is the more correct of the two. He supposes, as it were, that the ostrich in sandy and warm places uses the earth as an incubator, thus giving evidence of intelligence rather than a want of caution or the lack of 'a parent's mind.' It is proved beyond question in the great ostrich farms of South Africa, where the ground is not suited to incubation, that the ostrich is possessed of highly developed maternal instincts;

indeed, both the cock and the hen take their proper share in the process of hatching the eggs, and woe be to any venturesome stranger who incautiously wanders too near their nest. At such a time the cock bird becomes a veritable fury, and one kick from his horned foot means certain disablement, and very probably death.

In addition to the fable of burying its head in the sand, the ostrich has derived its character of stupidity from its habit of swallowing large solid substances to assist its digestion. Of this habit very much might be said. Buffon declares that they would eat pieces of 'red-hot iron' in small quantities; and the Arabs are serious in believing that their staple diet consists of stones and bits of iron. Cuvier states that in the stomach of an ostrich he discovered that not only were pieces of iron "worn away as they would likely be by trituration against other hard bodies, but they had been considerably reduced by some digestive juice, and presented all the evidence of actual corrosion." Dr. Shaw says that he has seen an ostrich swallow bullets which came hot from the mold. That ostriches do actually swallow, and seem to appreciate, pieces of iron and brass I have had the opportunity of proving to my own satisfaction.

While strolling near a large ostrich farm in Cape Colony a few years ago, I thought that, as the chance presented itself, I would put to the test the stories I had read as a youngster respecting the 'digestion of an ostrich,' one of my earliest books on natural history having contained some of the stories I have mentioned above. There happened to be at that moment a grand cock bird in brilliant black and white plumage standing close to the railings of the farm. Taking some brass military buttons from my pocket, I threw them, one by one into the enclosure. To my delight, this 'steel digesting bird' lowered his snake-like neck and swallowed them, then looked up for more. I threw him a brass military badge, such as soldiers wear on their collars, and this he also consumed with the same apparent relish. Then, a young soldier who was with me, thinking to set the ostrich a task beyond his power, offered it part of a broken pocketknife. To our amazement the ostrich accepted the gift with the same appreciation he had shown in disposing of the buttons and badge, and we began to wonder why he did not swallow the railings and obtain his liberty. Whether he lived to digest the substantial odds and ends we had given him I cannot say, but that he actually swallowed them with apparent enjoyment and a desire 'for more' there cannot be the least doubt; my own eyes were my proof.

Much more might be written here about the ostrich, for Arab lore is full of fables concerning it: that it is the progeny of a camel and a bird- hence the ancient name Struthio camelus; that it never drinks water; throws stones at its assailants, and so on; but enough space has already been devoted to this one species, and we have many others yet to notice.

There is the old tradition which tells us that the Bittern makes 'the quagmire reel' by thrusting its long bill in the mud and using it as a kind of musical instrument. Hence it derives its name of 'mere drum.'

"And the bittern sounds his drum
Booming from the sedgy shallows"
-Scott.

"As a bitore bumbleth in the mire."
-Chaucer.

Thomson, adopting the old-time error for the purposes of poetry, writes:

"So that scarce
The bittern knows his time with bill engulfed

SUPERSTITIONS ABOUT ANIMALS

To shake the sounding marsh."

The Hoopoe is not a British bird, but as it is sometimes seen in this country, it will not be out of place to mention it briefly here. There are few birds which are credited with more curious attributes and regarded with more superstition than the hoopoe. "The Arabs have a superstitious reverence for it," says Dr. Tristram, "and believing it to possess marvelous medicinal qualities, they call it the 'doctor bird.' Its head is an indispensable ingredient in all their charms, and in the practice of witchcraft. They also believe that it listens to whispers and betrays secrets, and, what is far more important, that it has the power of detecting water and of pointing out hidden wells and springs. These attributes have doubtless been suggested by the quaint and grotesque movements of its head and tall crest, which it erects in walking, and then, with solemn, portentous look, it bends its head down till the bill touches the ground, raising and depressing the crest at the same time."

Gilbert White mentions the stately deportment of these pretty birds in his entertaining Natural History:

"The most unusual birds I ever observed in these parts were a pair of hoopoes (upupa), which came several years ago in the summer, and frequented an ornamental piece of ground which joins to my garden for some weeks. They used to march about in a stately manner, feeding in the walks, many times in the day; and seemed disposed to breed in my outlet; but were frighted and persecuted by idle boys, who would never let them be at rest."

On the Continent the hoopoe is the bird "upon whose head stands a crested plume," into which, says the ancient fable, King Tereus was transformed for his cruelty to trustful Philomela.

SUPERSTITIONS ABOUT ANIMALS

There still exist in some of the more remote country districts quaint old superstitions about Bees which are not without a certain beauty and romance. One of these superstitions is that when a death takes place in the house to which the bees belong, information must be formally given to the bees, or they will forsake their hives. Consequently a member of the family takes the door-key of the house, and, tapping three times upon the hives with it, seriously makes known to the busy little creatures the sad bereavement which has taken place. Thereupon the bees, having listened to the deputation and mentally made a note of the sad demise, resolve that as the melancholy incident was not caused by undue negligence, and they have been properly informed of it by an accredited representative, they will continue to fill their storehouses as if nothing had happened. On the day of the funeral the hives are draped with black cloth or crape, and in better-class families, who are not educated sufficiently to be entirely free from superstition, wine and cake are set apart for the bees, so that they may, as recognized mourners, take a full share in the family grief. Similarly, when a wedding takes place, the bees are properly informed of the interesting event, and take a fair share in the general rejoicing, their hives being decorated with red, which, under the circumstances, superstitious bee-keepers consider a more suitable color than black. Not only in regard to funerals and weddings are the bees given information of events which are taking place, but in all matters of serious importance to their owners they are supplied with all the news that is considered important.

"Londoners can hardly realize that superstitions about bird and beast are as rife in country places as they were in Shakespeare's day," says a writer in a northern daily paper. "A Bedfordshire woman was telling me the other day, says a correspondent, how her son had been stung all over by bees. 'And no other wonder,' she said; 'he never told them he was

going to put them in a new 'ome, and everybody knows that
before you goes to put bees in a new 'ome you must knock three
times on the top of the 'ive, and tell 'em same as you must tell
'em when any one dies in the 'ouse. Ef you don't, they'll be
spiteful, for bees is understanding creatures, an' knows what you
say to them."

In a charming and pathetic poem called 'Telling the
Bees,' Whittier very poetically describes the old English custom
which has been referred to above, a custom which has also, it
appears, been introduced into America. After a month's absence
('to love- a year) a lover returns to Fernside Farm, the home of
his sweetheart:

"Just the same as a month before,-
The house and the trees,
The barn's brown gable, the vine by the door,
Nothing changed but the hive of bees.

Before them, under the garden wall,
Forward and back.
Went drearily singing the chore-girl small.
Draping each hive with a shred of black.

Trembling I listened : the summer sun
Had the chill of snow;
For I knew she was telling the bees of one
Gone on the journey we all must go!

Then I said to myself, 'My Mary weeps
For the dead to-day:
Haply her blind old grandsire sleeps
The fret and the pain of his age away.'

But her dog whined low; on the doorway sill,

SUPERSTITIONS ABOUT ANIMALS

With his cane to his chin,
The old man sat; and the chore-girl still
Sung to the bees stealing out and in.

And the song she was singing ever since
In my ear sounds on
'Stay at home, pretty bees, fly not hence!
Mistress Mary is dead and gone!'"

Another notion respecting bees is that when a farmer's hive dies it will not be long before he himself is compelled to remove from his farm. This belief is not without an element of truth, for a hive of bees rarely dies unless the season is so bad that it is disastrous to farming; consequently, where a farmer holds his farm on a yearly tenancy, it may follow that he will find it necessary to go elsewhere to build up his fortune.

It is a strange coincidence that people who dwell in the country and have the best opportunities of observing the habits of birds and animals in their natural surroundings are more superstitious about them than dwellers in towns. Even at the present day, as we have already noticed, there linger, among the older people and in remote country districts, many curious ideas which a little personal investigation of the subject lying close at hand would promptly and entirely dispel. But to go to country people for a knowledge of natural history is very much like going to Londoners for information respecting the National Gallery, Westminster Abbey, or the British Museum; in either case one would be surprised at the lack of cognition and even of ordinary interest. Quite recently I heard of a country woman who was afraid to cross a common after dark 'for fear of the Death's-head moths stinging her;' and, besides newts, there are many creatures which are invested, in the vulgar imagination, with the power of stinging- lizards, for instance: "Their softest touch as smart as lizards' stings!"

SUPERSTITIONS ABOUT ANIMALS

The frail, harmless, little Shrew-mouse is another animal which country people have for centuries regarded with aversion. Poor mite! it is not only harmless, it is useful, timid, weak, and was honored by the Egyptians with a place among their sacred animals. But among country people the shrew has always had a bad name, and it has not altogether been lost in the advance of learning. This may be in some degree due to its offensive odor. In any case, the unfortunate pygmy is credited with being able to inflict a poisonous bite, and what is worse, with causing suffering to animals, and even the rotting of a limb by crawling over it. Much more so formerly than now, animals that were stiff in the joints or lame were said to be 'shrew-struck,' which meant simply that a shrew-mouse had run over the affected parts. Ridiculous as this superstition was, the cure for the malady was equally ridiculous. This consisted of applying a 'shrew-ash' to the part which had been injured, and a 'shrew-ash' was practically 'a hair of the dog.' It was made by boring a hole in an ash-tree, inserting therein a shrew-mouse, sealing the hole with a wooden peg, and leaving the miserable little creature to die in its prison. The tree in which this cruel interment had taken place was then called a 'shrew ash,' and so long as the tree remained a tree any twig of it placed on a 'shrew-struck' horse, cow, dog, or any other animal would prove an effectual remedy. White mentions that near the church at Selborne "there stood, about twenty years ago, a very old, grotesque hollow pollard ash, which for ages had been looked on with no small veneration as 'a shrew-ash.'" The previous vicar, however, had a mind above such simple ignorance, and therefore, "regardless of the remonstrances of the bystanders, who interceded in vain for its preservation, urging its power and efficacy," he had it destroyed.

A similar character has been given to the Gecko, a species of lizard which is found in Palestine and Egypt. The natives implicitly believe that the gecko produces leprous sores by crawling over a person's body. Not only is this belief an utter fallacy, but it is moreover without any reasonable foundation, for the gecko is quite a harmless and inoffensive reptile. It is, however, a strikingly ugly animal, moves without the slightest noise, and is nocturnal in its wanderings. Probably these characteristics, together with the harsh 'clucking' sound, from which it derives its name, have given rise to the unjust charges that have been brought against it. Quite as inaccurate and unwarranted as the superstitions of the shrew-mouse and gecko is the supposition that the Goatsucker, or Night-jar, drains milk from the udders of cows and goats, a supposition which, however, is common wherever the birds are to be found. Nor is this the only evil practice with which the goatsucker is charged: it is also said to infect cows with a fatal malady called puckeridge.

This, of course, is quite an erroneous idea. The malady is caused by an insect which lays its eggs along the chine of cattle, where the maggots when hatched eat their way beneath the hide and grow to a very large size. Similarly, in some hot climates there is a small insect called the jigger which burrows under the skin of people's feet, causing intense pain, gangrene, and, if a remedy is not quickly found, even death itself. There are other superstitions connected with the goatsucker, each of which stamp it as a bird of ill repute. The worst charge against it is that it will attack young children, which, perhaps it is unnecessary to explain, has no foundation in fact. The goatsucker, like the swallow, is insectivorous, and therefore a bird which should be prized and protected. Unlike the swallow, however, it is a bird of nocturnal habits, and no doubt this fact, together with its noiseless, ghost-like flight, as in the case of the owl, has given rise to the superstition that it is a bird of evil propensities and to be feared.

Referring to the goatsucker's reputation for gorging itself on milk without making payment in return, reminds me that the adder and hedgehog have also obtained the same notoriety. By what method they commit this act of pilfering I have not been informed, but nature does not appear to have constructed any of the three creatures with a view of their carrying out the duties of dairymaid in their own interest. Perhaps the adder is supposed to adopt the same ingenious scheme as that of a wonderful lizard which, A Survey of the Wisdom of God tells us, lives in many parts of Lower Egypt. The description of this lizard, and its acrobatic method of obtaining a drink, are well worth reading:

"It resembles a crocodile, only that it is but three or four feet long, and lives wholly on the land. As it is exceeding fond of the milk of ewes and she-goats, it makes use of a remarkable expedient. It twists its long tail round the leg of the ewe or goat, and so sucks her at his leisure."

A truly marvelous animal, and one which I should like to see during its business hours! But what is the goat or ewe doing meanwhile? As a contrast to these superstitions, it is pleasing to know that while so many creatures are supposed to be able to inflict injury on people or other animals, or commit acts of pilfering, farmers are quite sure that the presence of Goats on a farm will keep away foot-disease. This is the sole reason for which goats are kept on many farms, but how they perform this kindly office I have not yet been informed. Quite recently I mentioned this superstition to a Yorkshire farmer, and though he himself did not keep a goat among his stock, he assured me that there was nothing superstitious about the custom, for it was well known that foot-disease will not appear among animals where a goat is kept. The truth of this assertion he was unable to prove by circumstances which had come under his own observation; and, indeed, it would be a very difficult matter to prove. Only by introducing a goat among animals suffering from the disease, and carefully noting the effect, could anything like the truth of the supposition be established or contradicted.

SUPERSTITIONS ABOUT ANIMALS

Turning to a superstition of quite another kind, it is a very common belief that Rats will leave a ship which is destined to become a wreck, or, as is sometimes said, "Rats will leave a sinking ship." But this is even more nonsensical than the other, for rats will also leave a burning building, a house which is being broken up, or any such kind of danger, so nervous are they of being damaged. Not long ago I read in a newspaper, the copy of which I have unfortunately lost, that on a certain night a colony of rats was seen coming from a vessel which was moored alongside a dock. They made their exodus by way of the hawser, and it was well for them they changed their habitation. The vessel, a few days later, put out to sea and was lost! That makes a really charming story, showing how much more clearly than men a certain despised and hunted animal may understand, and even anticipate, the mysterious dispensations of Providence! But rats will have to 'look to their laurels.' Cats are entering as competitors in this field of presentiment, and are likely to turn the rats out altogether.

An account was given in 1901 of two cats which unmistakably gave warning of the accident that happened to the torpedo-destroyer Salmon- at any rate, so said some influential papers after the occurrence. As the story goes, the Salmon and another vessel named the Sturgeon were lying side by side in harbor. On the former "dwelt two cats, who were the special pets of the crew, and who had never been known to show the smallest inclination to desert. But on this particular morning, in spite of being chased by the crew and worried by the dog, the cats never faltered in their determination to get off the Salmon and on to the Sturgeon, and when the first-named destroyer had weighed anchor for what was to prove the disastrous voyage, the cats made one last spring as the vessels separated, and landed themselves on the Sturgeon's deck."

There! After this instance of feline presentiment, any

persons who get shipwrecked have only themselves to blame. All they have to do to discover whether their voyage will be prosperous or otherwise is to take a cat on board and pin their welfare on its behavior. If the cat curls comfortably in front of the cabin fire, all will be well; if it persists in jumping ashore, "in spite of being chased by the crew and worried by the dog," their salvation depends on jumping ashore after the cat.

There is a very pretty superstition among children that the gaudy little insect which is commonly known as the Ladybird, or Ladycow, is easily frightened on being told that a catastrophe has happened to her home. This is a very quaint and childlike notion, and is mentioned here only because it seems to be known in every country where the ladybird is found. The custom among children is to take one of the little insects in their hand and sing to it a pathetic ditty which, so far as I can quote it from memory, is usually worded:

"Ladybird, ladybird, fly away home.
Your house is on fire, and your children are gone."

And when the ditty comes to an end, and the ladybird is tossed into the air, the children suppose that the frightened little creature flies away to her 'home' in terrible anguish, expecting to find it enveloped in flames, and her offspring burned to death. All this is very pretty and childlike in its innocence, and is a kind of notion which only very precise and unromantic people would wish to see superseded by plain matters of fact. Let the little ones keep their innocent imagination as long as they are able, for all too soon the charming days of frightened ladybirds and fairies and Santa Claus pass away, and prosaic, unromantic reality takes their place. While walking on the outskirts of Odessa, during a tour in Russia, with a friend who was born in that city, I came across a group of children who were raising their hands in the air and chanting a peculiar tune which I took to be some national hymn. Being interested in the actions of the children, and not understanding the language, I asked my friend for an explanation, and he replied, "Oh, they are singing that song about the ladybird."

There is no more beautiful or more poetic story of any animal than how the Donkey was given the dark cross-shaped mark upon its back. When Christ was about to make His entry into Jerusalem, so tradition says. He chose an ass in preference to any other beast of burden, because it was a meek and humble creature and best suited to carry one who 'made Himself of no reputation.' But so that it might for ever more be known that God Himself had ridden upon the beast. He caused a dark cross to appear upon its back, typifying the kind of death He died. Similarly, it is said that the dark spot on a haddock represents the mark made by Peter's thumb when he took the fish out of the sea to obtain the tribute money. It would be a pity to spoil this pretty notion by suggesting that the haddock was not the fish which the disciples found so useful at a time of special need.

The question now arises as to whether I shall conclude this section of my subject with the two foregoing pretty fables, or finish it with some remarks on that familiar butt 'and bone of contention the Sea-serpent. If I deal with the subject here, many will say that I should have inserted it in the next division, 'Creatures of the Imagination;' but were I to do so, others would at once say the sea serpent is no creature of the imagination, it is a reptile which has an actual existence, and a belief in its corporeality should not be treated as superstition. In this dilemma I shall take the course of writing upon the subject straight away. Of the sea-serpent very much might be written. This is also equally true of any other subject about which little or nothing is known. That the animal has any actual existence as a serpent is very doubtful, but that a marine monster of gigantic proportions more or less solid, and called by the name of "sea serpent," is a reality there seems to be ample evidence to believe.

Many persons who could have no ulterior motive in creating fairy-tales emphatically assert that they have seen such a monster, and have gone so far as to give graphic and minute details of its appearance. Not only once, but on several occasions, the whole of a ship's crew has been terrified by the appearance of some 'great denizen of the deep,' to which they have given the common name of sea-serpent, and not only have they given a realistic description of the awful monster, but they have even gone so far as to make a sketch of it- presumably after it had disappeared. Why should these men put themselves to the trouble of concocting a yarn about these creatures? Why should they deliberately set to work to combine in foisting a lie upon the public? What benefit could they possibly derive from such a course beyond a moment's notoriety? True, it may be suggested that the men were honest but mistaken. That is, however, merely a matter of opinion, and in no way helps to solve the problem.

There have been sea serpents innumerable. The ancients told many strange stories of great serpents which lived in the ocean, and now and again, crawling upon the land, caused fearful havoc before they retired to their proper element. Such were the monsters which at the siege of Troy came up from the sea and crushed to death Laocoon and his two sons. Coming, however, to modern times, we have plenty of material to use in a chapter on sea serpents; but only one or two of the many monsters which have been described at various times can be mentioned here. In 1752 a marine monster answering to the accepted likeness of a sea-serpent was seen and sketched, and a full description of the animal, together with its likeness, was put into print. In 1848 also, the same serpent, or one of its family, was seen by the officers and crew of H.M.S. Dcedalus, who gave a clear description of the monster they had seen. A few years later. Captain Harrington, of the Castilian, also saw the 'serpent,' and sent a detailed report of his observation to the Board of Trade bearing his own signature and those of his chief officers. In 1898 still another 'serpent' was seen by the whole of the crew of a Dundee vessel, and their description of it, together with a sketch made on the spot, appeared in the daily papers. And now quite recently yet another monster has been sighted and graphically described. Let us take the description of two of these monsters and compare them. First, the 'serpent' seen by Captain Harrington and the crew of the Castilian:

"While myself and officers were standing on the lee side of the poop looking towards the Island of St. Helena, we were startled by the sight of a huge marine animal, which reared its head out of the water within twenty yards of the ship; when it suddenly disappeared for about half a minute, and then reappeared, showing us distinctly its neck and head about ten or twelve feet out of the water. Its head was shaped like a long nun-buoy, and I suppose the diameter to have been seven or eight feet in the largest part, with a kind of scroll or tuft of loose skin encircling it about two feet from the top. The water was discolored for several hundred feet from its head; so much so, that on its first appearance my impression was that the ship was in broken water produced by some volcanic agency. But the second appearance completely dispelled these fears, and assured us that it was a monster of extraordinary length which appeared to be moving slowly towards the land. The ship was going too fast to enable us to reach the masthead in time to form a correct estimate of its length; but from what we saw from the deck, we conclude that it must have been over two hundred feet long. I am convinced that it belonged to the serpent tribe. It was of a dark color about the head, and was covered with several spots."

Now let us notice the description of the monster seen by the captain and crew of the Dundee vessel Dart, in 1898:

SUPERSTITIONS ABOUT ANIMALS

"It resembled nothing we could describe nearer than the ancient animals of prehistoric existence that we sometimes find described and illustrated by scientific men. Altogether it must have been 180 feet long. The head was of a long tapering shape. The mouth being open, we saw the full size of it. It must have been large enough to swallow at least a cow or a horse. The teeth shone in the faint light, and gave the animal a terrifying appearance. A long flipper-like appendage seemed to dangle from its body about fifteen or twenty feet from its head. The eyes shone with a green light, shifting from green to blue and often crimson, and drove terror into our hearts. Its body had a mane like a fin running down the full length of the back and breast. It was of a dark color, and unlike any monster we in a natural way could have dreamed of."

In the face of such minute details as these, certified in each case by several signatures, it would be idle to assert that the crews were under a total misapprehension. It is evident they saw that 'something' which has obtained the popular name of sea-serpent. Both accounts describe the creature as 'a monster,' and after reading them we feel little inclined to envy the men who were favored with a glimpse of it. But the two descriptions, separated as they are by a break of forty years, have much more in common than a simple allusion to the serpent as 'a monster.'

In several details they bear a striking similarity. One monster, we are told, had a head shaped like 'a long nun-buoy', the others' head was of 'a long tapering shape.' One had 'a kind of scroll or tuft of loose skin encircling it about two feet from the top', the other had 'a flipper-like appendage,' which 'seemed to dangle about fifteen or twenty feet from its head.' One was 'over two hundred feet long;' the other 'must have been 180 feet long.' Each of the monsters was of 'a dark color,' and both were near enough to the vessels to be seen distinctly one 'within twenty yards,' the other so close that the crew could see the full size of its open mouth. Of course, it must be understood that in comparing two descriptions of a marine monster they will not tally in detail, especially in the matter of figures.

We can fully understand that when an animal of 'fearful and terrifying appearance' makes its appearance suddenly alongside a ship, the crew are not to be expected to measure the monster with any exactness. Taking this into consideration, the two descriptions have very much in common. What these apparitions were, however, may always remain a mystery. That they were sea monsters having a real existence I personally have no doubt. We may laugh at the old stories of travelers landing on the back of a sea-serpent and hoisting a Union Jack under the impression that they were 'annexing' another new colony for the Crown, but we cannot so easily dispose of such detailed and properly attested descriptions as the foregoing; neither must we be too positive that we know of the existence of every animal which inhabits the deep sea.

Numerous have been the attempts made to explain away sea-serpents- a school of porpoises, sharks, floating seaweed, a devil-fish trailing its long limbs behind it, a water-spout- these are among the efforts to solve the problem; but those who have been among the fortunate few to obtain a glimpse of the mysterious monsters declare that none of these explanations will fully meet the case, and certainly they do not explain away the two monsters described above. We, therefore, who have not been so fortunate as to see a sea-serpent for ourselves must patiently reserve our criticism until such time as one is harpooned and towed into harbor.

SUPERSTITIONS ABOUT ANIMALS

CREATURES OF THE IMAGINATION

"Far away in the twilight-time
Of every people, in every clime,
Dragons, and griffins, and monsters dire,
Born of water, and air, and fire,
Or nursed, like the python, in the mud
And ooze of the old Deucalion flood,
Crawl and wriggle and foam with rage
Through dusk tradition and ballad age."
-Whittier.

However great a part imagination has played in crediting certain members of the animal kingdom with attributes and powers which they do not possess, the height of superstition is reached in the belief in monstrosities and creatures which have never had any real existence. The origin of most of these fabulous animals is lost in the dim reaches of antiquity, and only vague guesses can be made in respect thereof. It may be safely assumed, however, that many of them have developed by a gradual process of exaggeration- much in the same way as the herring on the beach became a whale. Others have been created by a direct effort of the imagination. Bottiger, in writing of that monster of antiquity the Griffin, says it was merely the creation of Indian tapestry-makers, but that the Greeks, seeing the tapestry at the court of the King of Persia, thought the animals depicted upon it were really inhabitants of India. It seems highly probable, therefore, that certain other fabulous animals have had a similar origin; while others again, such as the cockatrice and the basilisk, owe their creation to an exaggerated idea of the power of serpents, consequent upon the utter loathing in which they are universally held. But it is not my intention here to endeavor to trace the origin of these creatures of the imagination. In respect of many of them the attempt would be futile, for, if I may so state the case, they have no beginning; they come up to us vaguely from the antediluvian age, a combined product of creation and imagination. Moreover, no good service could be rendered by such an effort. It will therefore be my purpose to deal only with such of the fabulous animals as I think are of special interest by reason of their prominence in our literature.

It is much to be regretted that several of these monstrosities have been permitted to enter the pages of Holy Scripture: in most instances the translation is an utter violation of the original. Of course the reason is not far to seek. In the days of the Authorized Version the creatures to which I am referring- the cockatrice, dragon, satyr, unicorn, and Others- were believed to have a real existence, and their place in our sacred writings came largely as a matter of course, but their presence there today creates a real difficulty.

The Revised Version of the Bible has gone very far towards removing this difficulty by giving to the animals wrongly translated their proper names; even now there are several passages which are in need of alteration. To any ordinary reader, the appearance in the sacred writings of creatures which are nowadays commonly known to have had no real existence is bewildering, and probably not a little unsettling. To such a reader my earnest advice is to study any good Natural History- such, for instance, as Dr. Tristram's, from which I have more than once quoted- and his difficulties will quickly be swept away. The creatures that have caused him so much perplexity- such as the dragon and the cockatrice- he will find are merely other names for animals with which he is, for the most part, quite familiar.

Basilisk and Cockatrice have now become interchangeable names for the same fabulous reptile, but originally they were distinct. The basilisk, or regulus of the ancients, was the king of all serpents; and, according to Pliny, was found in the African deserts, where it would appear to be a veritable despot. All other snakes fled from its awful presence with horrified precipitation; and even the flowers and fruits perished when touched by the poisonous fumes of its scorching breath.

> "What shield of Ajax could avoid their death,
> By th' basilisk, whose pestilential breath
> Doth pierce firm marble, and whose baneful ey
> Wounds with a glance so that the soundest dy?"

Its progression was majestic in the extreme. It held itself erect, not trailing its body as in the manner of other serpents. Its eyes were red and fiery, its face pointed, and upon its head, as token of its sovereignty, it wore a crown. Shelley tells us that its skin was 'green and golden,' but these colors are apparently chosen for the sake of euphony, and not from any intention to describe the reptile accurately. Far otherwise, however, is the desire of the sagacious naturalist whose opinions on several matters of natural history I have introduced into this volume. He plunges boldly into the description of an animal which exists only in imagination, and his description, to make matters worse, is plagiaristic:

"The cockatrice, or basilisk, is a kind of serpent of a reddish colour, and has a thick body, fiery eyes, and a sharp head, on which it wears a crest that looks like a crown. It has the honour to be called the king of serpents, because of its crown and majestic pace; and also because all other serpents are said to fly from its presence with dread The cockatrice in its motion lifts its head and the fore part of its body upwards, the middle and hinder parts only touching the ground. Its poison is said to be so extremely strong, that if any person is bitten by the serpent death speedily takes place."

SUPERSTITIONS ABOUT ANIMALS

It is curious how so many writers who undertake a description of a serpent portray the reptile as having a 'crest.' Here are a few out of many:

"As when some peasant in a bushy brake,
Has with unwary footing press'd a snake;
He starts aside, astonished when he spies.
His rising crest, blue neck and rolling eyes."
Dryden (Virgil's Aenid.)

"He, bolder now, uncall'd before her stood,
But as in gaze admiring; oft he bow'd
His turret crest, and sleek enamell'd neck.
Fawning; and lick'd the ground whereon she trod."
-Milton.

"The eagle, faint with pain and toil.
Remitted his strong flight, and near the sea
Languidly fluttered, hopeless so to foil
His adversary, who then reared on high
His red and burning crest, radiant with victory."
-Shelley.

"Soon he reached the fiery serpents
With their blazing crests uplifted."
-Longfellow.

The idea of a 'crest' has very probably arisen from the 'hood' or inflation of the neck, which is a marked feature of some species of snakes when in a state of excitement. There is no kind of snake that wears a crest such as is described by the poets mentioned above, in association with the regal power of the basilisk. This fact does not, however, prevent the author of the book I have just mentioned from publishing an illustration of the basilisk wearing its crown with proper kingly dignity. The author in this instance has not been satisfied with describing the reptile as being 'the king of serpents because of its crown,' but he goes to the extreme of illustrating the creature with a woodcut, in which we see it with pointed nose, head raised aloft, coils of body typifying 'majestic pace,' and a solid kingly crown, such as the school-book pictures of our kings have made familiar, perched in a consequential way upon its head.

The terrible power of killing people by the glare of its eyes, which the ancients attributed to the basilisk, is mentioned several times in the works of Shakespeare:

> "Here take this too,
> It is a basilisk unto mine eye."
> -Cymbeline.

> "Come basilisk, and kill the innocent gazer with thy sight."
> -Henry VI.

> "Would they were basilisks to strike thee dead."
> -Richard III.

It should be understood that the fabulous animal mentioned here, and frequently met with in early writings, is not the South American lizard of the same name. The Cockatrice, which we now understand to be the same fabulous reptile as the basilisk, superstition tells us was produced from a 'cock's egg hatched by a frog!' Could imagination possibly have concocted anything more ludicrous? In appearance it is said to differ in no respect from the basilisk, and it is credited with the same terrible power of killing people by its gaze:

SUPERSTITIONS ABOUT ANIMALS

"Let them feel the utmost of your crueltyes;
And kill with looks as cockatrices doo."
-Spenser.

"Here with a cockatrice' dead killing eye
He raises up himself and makes a pause.
-Shakespeare (Lucrece.)

"A cockatrice hast thou hatch'd to the world
Whose unavoided eye is murderous,"
-Shakespeare (Richard III.)

The cockatrice is frequently mentioned in Holy Scripture, and always as a reptile of extreme malignity:

"Out of the serpent's root shall come forth a cockatrice, and his fruit shall be a fiery flying serpent.
-Isaiah.

"They hatch cockatrice' eggs, and weave the spider's web; he that eateth of their eggs dieth, and that which is crushed breaketh out into a viper."
-Isaiah.

"Behold, I will send serpents, cockatrices, among you, which will not be charmed, and they shall bite you, saith the Lord."
-Jeremiah.

It is quite evident that the writers of these and other passages where the word occurs wished to depict some reptile of more than ordinary malignity and venomousness. In the margin of the first two of the above passages we find the words 'or adder'; but the adder is comparatively tame and innocuous when compared with the terrible reptile described by the sacred writers. In one of the quotations from the book of Isaiah, the writer speaks of an egg which being 'crushed breaketh out into a viper.' This passage in no way helps us; rather the reverse, for a viper is a viviparous reptile. The root-word from which the fabulous cockatrice is taken is also ambiguous, meaning simply 'to hiss.' If we turn to the Revised Version in the hope of finding the difficulty overcome, we are led into a still deeper perplexity, for the revisers have simply substituted one fabulous reptile for another; they have merely altered 'cockatrice' to 'basilisk.' Far better would it have been to translate the root-word into the name of one of the several venomous snakes which are found in Egypt and Palestine- the cobra, the horned cerastes, or, more particularly, on account of its size and extreme venomousness, the daboia. It is highly probable that the last-named snake is that which the sacred writers wished to describe- the snake 'which will not be charmed.'

Every nation has its own particular Dragon, or if it has not a dragon it has a kind of national pet in the form of some traditional monster much after the same type. Go where you will you will find the brute. Its ugly form can be seen on the Chinese standards as well as on our own coins; its ancient haunts are pointed out in nearly every corner of the globe; there are dragons' caves and dragons' hills and dragons' mountains innumerable. It figures under some name or other in every literature- it is in our own Bible. It was worshiped in Babylonia in the days of that empire's greatness, and as far east as China and India. It is such an ancient beast that its birth is lost in the mists of antiquity; but it is also so modern that it constantly appears as a popular character in children's books, and its ugly figure is cunningly used to beautify wares of pottery. There is no getting rid of the dragon. Most ancient of beasts, he is still the most modern, and will be the most lasting. And yet he is only a fabulous brute- a type, a figure. He represents the power of evil, and wherever we hear traditional tales of him we find that there is another type in contrast, the power of good, which goes forth to overcome him- the conflict of Evil with Good, and Good always gains the victory. Such is the story of the fair maiden of Drachenfels (or Dragon-field). Once upon a time, so the story goes, there lived a monstrous snake (or dragon), which wrought such havoc in this district on the Rhine that the pure white maiden went forth from the castle in all her loveliness and innocence to slay the brute. And the victory of St. George, our patron saint, the rescue of Andromeda by the valiant Perseus, Apollo's triumph over the malignant serpent- all these are but versions of one common legend, and all have their source in the Hindu myth of Krishna, who tore in pieces the body of the black and evil serpent which, concealed in the great river, had poisoned all who drank thereof.

And can we not go back to Genesis and find there the fount from which all these legends have sprung? "I will put enmity between thee and the woman, and between thy seed and her seed; it shall bruise thy head, and thou shalt bruise his heel." And then may we not go to the Mount of Calvary, and in the overwhelming tragedy of the Cross find there the consummation of all that these myths and legends have, by a mysterious intuition, been anticipating and depicting from time immemorial? Are not the words, 'It is finished!' but the idealism of Krishna's bloody hands and Apollo's swift sword? The victory was won! "And he laid hold on the dragon, that old serpent, which is the Devil, and Satan, and bound him a thousand years. And cast him into the bottomless pit, and shut him up, and set a seal upon him, that he should deceive the nations no more, till the thousand years should be fulfilled: and after that he must be loosed a little season."

It is not to be wondered at that when dragon worship and dragon legends have been almost world-spread, dragons under various forms should have found their way into Holy Writ. In the passage I have just quoted from the Apocalypse we have the dragon as we find it in the legends I have referred to- a symbol of Evil which is finally overcome by the power of Righteousness. But in the Old Testament the word 'dragon' is used variously to represent an animal which inhabits desert places, an aquatic monster, a large land reptile, and a serpent. In the first connection, 'dragon' now appears in the Revised Version of the Old Testament as 'jackal,' which from its habit of frequenting 'waste places,' of 'wailing,' and of 'snuffing up the wind,' is without doubt the creature which the sacred writers intended to represent. In the passages where the name 'dragon' is applied to an inhabitant of the deep the revisers have adopted the plan of retaining the old translation and adding a marginal note, 'or sea monsters.' There are, however, exceptions to this, as in Isaiah xxvii.:

"He shall slay the dragon that is in the sea."

In the passage:

"The young lion and the dragon shalt thou trample under feet." (Psalm xci/)

The word 'dragon' has been altered to 'serpent'; but in Deuteronomy xxxii., in a verse most obviously dealing with serpents of a deadly nature: "Their wine is the poison of dragons, and the cruel venom of asps," 'dragons' is retained without any marginal comment whatever.

It is not easy to understand why the revisers should alter the text in some instances and not in others. When dealing with animals which have had a real existence, and with which the writers themselves were doubtlessly conversant, it would have been better to render the text a little vague rather than retain the name of a monster that every one knows is entirely imaginary. I have not thought it necessary to quote a description of this legendary monster. The finest I have read, and one which I think cannot be beaten, is Spenser's (Book I., Canto xi.).

The Unicorn is another creature which, in its generally recognized form, is simply a freak of the imagination; but the ancients implicitly believed in the real existence of the animal, and frequent references are made to it in their writings. Ctesias said unicorns had white bodies, red heads, blue eyes, and on their foreheads grew a single horn a cubit and a half long. "Drinking cups are formed of these, and those who drink out of them are said to be subject neither to spasm, nor epilepsy, nor to the effect of poison." Ctesias said he himself had seen the horn, which was very heavy and red; but he did not venture to say he had seen the beast itself. Pliny called the animal a monoceros, and described it as having the head of a stag, the body of a horse, the feet of an elephant, and the tail of a wild boar, and it had a single horn two cubits long projecting from the center of its forehead. In describing the same animal, Aelian says it was as big as a full-grown horse, with a mane and yellow woolly hair of greatest softness, with feet like the elephant, and the tail of the wild boar. Its horn was black, growing between the eyebrows, and was not smooth, but had natural twistings and a sharp point.

It seems highly probable that the horn which these writers and 'old Father Aristotle' had seen was the horn or tooth of the Narwhal, which was highly prized by the ancients, and was called the tooth of the unicorn. The description as given above fairly represents the horn of a narwhal which once belonged to me, though the measurements are considerably less. The narwhal's tooth was superstitiously supposed to possess the virtue of preventing poison taking effect, and we are told that Charles IX., fearful of being treacherously poisoned, was in the habit of placing in his wine-cup a piece of the 'unicorn's tooth' to counteract the effect of any poison inserted therein. It is pretty much after the description of the animal given above that the unicorn now appears as the left-hand supporter of our British coat-of-arms. Frequent references are made in the Old Testament to a creature called a unicorn, and in all instances it represents an animal of great strength and ferocity, but strangely enough an animal possessing more than one horn:

> "He hath as it were the strength of an unicorn."
> -Numbers.

> "Will the unicorn be willing to serve thee, or abide by thy crib?"
> -Job.

> "His horns are like the horns of unicorns: with them he shall push the people together to the ends of the earth."
> -Deuteronomy.

> "Save me from the lion's mouth: for thou hast heard me from the horns of the unicorns."
> -Psalms.

There is every reason to suppose that the animal which the Old Testament writers intended should be recognized in the above passages was the Reem, a species of wild-ox which was formerly abundant all over Palestine, and indeed all over Europe, including our own islands. It was a beast of immense strength and great length of horn. To the Romans it was known as the Urus, to the old Germans as the Aurochs, but has now practically been hunted out of existence.

> "I clothed myself in thick hunting-clothes
> Fit for the chase of the urox or buffle."
> -Browning.

SUPERSTITIONS ABOUT ANIMALS

In the Revised Version the word 'unicorn' has in every instance been altered to 'wild-ox.' There is still another fabulous creature which has found its way into Holy Scripture without any adequate reason, that is the Satyr. The Satyrs in Greek and Roman mythology were a race of woodland divinities who are invariably associated with the worship of Bacchus. They were popularly supposed to be the offspring of Mercury and Iphthime, or of the naiads, and were ugly, animal-like creatures with flat noses, large ears, and horns upon their foreheads. How came these hideous creatures, then, into the book of Isaiah?

"Their houses shall be full of doleful creatures; and owls shall dwell there, and satyrs shall dance there."

"The wild beasts of the desert shall also meet with the wild beasts of the island, and the satyr shall cry to his fellow."

The marginal notes to these passages in the Revised Version give the alternative of regarding the satyrs as 'he-goats,' which is the meaning of the original; but the surroundings in which the 'he goats' are placed, their dancing and crying, seem to suggest that some other creature is intended. When we turn to Leviticus we find that the same word is translated 'devils,' and it is not improbable that Isaiah wished to describe some fabulous creature or other, which, according to the popular belief of the times, inhabited all ruins and waste places. This view is made stronger by the fact that in the second of the above passages, if we continue the reading, we find that together with the satyr is Lilith the night-monster, a fabulous bird similar to our 'night-crow,' or 'night-raven,' of which I shall have more to say later. The question is, however, a difficult one to decide. Another view is, that baboons and not he-goats are the animals which the prophet wished to describe, and, from his reference to their 'dancing' and 'crying,' this translation is just as likely as the other.

SUPERSTITIONS ABOUT ANIMALS

In South Africa I have many times watched these sportive animals leaping and gamboling among the rocks, or, as Isaiah puts it, 'dancing,' and have listened to their wild sounds of 'ba-hoo, ba-hoo,' as they 'cried to their fellows.' The desolation of Babylon and Idumea would be precisely the kind of l6nely surroundings they would delight in. Leaving the fabulous animals of the Bible, we now come to the Phoenix. Perhaps no other fabulous creature has given more opportunity for poetic imagery than this remarkable bird. Poetry abounds with references to it; the Roman emperors stamped its figure upon their coins, typifying a new and glorious era under their rule; preachers use it as a symbol of immortality, the death of the human body, and its resurrection to a perfect and eternal life; a well-known insurance society has chosen it as its emblem, and portrays the wonderful bird in lurid colors proceeding from the midst of brilliant smoke and flame. This bird is said to have been a native of Arabia. In appearance it was like an eagle, but its plumage was brilliant with red and gold. According to one account, it came to Egypt every five hundred years to the sanctuary dedicated to it there. The bird is said by ancient writers to have appeared four times in Egypt, the last visit being under Tiberius in the year 34 a.d.:

> "To all the fowls he seems
> A phoenix, gazed by all, as that sole bird
> When, to enshrine his relics in the sun's
> Bright temple, to Egyptian Thebes flies."
> -Milton.

In the shrine of the temple it placed the body of its dead parent, enclosed in a large egg made of myrrh. When it felt its own end drawing near, it built itself a nest, to which it gave the power of generation, so that when its own demise had taken place another phoenix might rise to a new life from the same nest. This is one of the several fables of the phoenix. Another is that a worm proceeded from the body of the dead bird and developed into another phoenix:

"Suddaine I beheld
Where, tumbling through the ayre in firie fold.
All flaming down she on the plaine was felde;
And soon her body turned to ashes colde.
I saw the foule, that doth the light despise.
Out of her dust like to a worm arise."
-Spenser.

But neither of these birds is quite the bird with which we have become familiar in picture and quotation. Our phoenix is a bird which, when grown to the age of five hundred years- a tolerably good age even for a fabulous bird- and conscious of its approaching death, built for itself a funeral pyre of choice woods and sweet-smelling gums, beat forth devouring flames with its wings, and, being consumed, rose from its own ashes resplendent in newness of life:

"My ashes, as the phoenix, may bring forth
A bird that will revenge upon you all."
-Shakespeare.

"And that which was of wonder most,
The phoenix left sweet Arable;
And on a caedar on this coast
Built up her tombe of spicerie.
As I conjectured by the same
Preparde to take her dying flame."
-Matthew Roydon.

"Sleep on, in visions of odours rest.
In balmier airs than ever yet stirr'd
Th' enchanted pile of that lonely bird,

SUPERSTITIONS ABOUT ANIMALS

Who sings at the last his own death lay.
And in music and perfume dies away."
-Moore.

"And glory, like the phoenix 'midst her fires,
Exhales her odours, blazes and expires."

"Behold her statue placed in glory's niche;
Her fetters burst, and just released from prison,
A virgin phoenix from her ashes risen."
-Byron.

"But when I am consumed with the Fire,
Give me new Phoenix-wings to fly at my desire."
-Keats.

"In death I thrive:
And like a Phenix re-aspire
From out my Narde, and Fun'rall fire."
-Herrick.

The Griffin, which, like its relative the dragon, has found a permanent place in English art, because of its adaptability to design, deserves a paragraph to itself. As I have already pointed out, the griffin was in the first place the creation of Indian tapestry workers, but being seen in their designs by Greeks at the Persian court, the griffin became firmly established as a creature having a real existence. So real was its existence, indeed, that the same ancient writers who were intrepid enough to describe the unicorn did not hesitate to give a description of the griffin. Ctesias says that the brute was so strong that it gained the victory over all other animals with the exception of the elephant and lion. In appearance it was very gorgeous. The feathers on its neck were blue and shining, its eyes were red and fiery, and it had the beak of an eagle, Aelian makes it a still more brilliant monster. The feathers on its back, he says, were black, those on its breast red, and it had white feathers upon its wings. The griffin was supposed to build its nest of solid gold in the mountains of India, which was its native place. It could be easily tamed- when taken very young! Though a native of India, the monster is alleged to have found its way to England- at least on one occasion. A man taking a walk, some centuries ago, in Leicestershire spied one of these terrible creatures stooping to drink at a pond, and tradition says that the man was very much upset. The place where the griffin was seen subsequently took its name from the monster, and the village to this day is called Griffidam.

The appearance of the griffin, according to our modern idea, as may be seen from the rearing monstrosity near the Law Courts, does not altogether coincide with the description given by ancient writers. It is now usually represented with the body, feet, and claws of a lion, the head and wings of an eagle, the ears of a horse, a stiff, bristling, fishlike mane, and feathers upon its back. It is precisely such a creature as a distorted mind might conjure up towards the early hours of the morning, or what might be the outcome of a deliberate intention to create something that was hideous and vile. John Bunyan succeeded brilliantly when he set to work to manufacture the monster Apollyon:

"The monster was most hideous to behold; it was clothed with scales like a fish (and they are his pride): he had wings like a dragon, feet like a bear, and out of his belly came forth fire and smoke, and his mouth was as the mouth of a lion."

Of a similar kind was the beast which appeared to St. John in his great vision at Patmos:

"A beast... having seven heads and ten horns, and upon his horns ten crowns... and the beast which I saw was like unto a leopard, and his feet were as the feet of a bear, and his mouth as the mouth of a lion."

No less horrible are the Harpies described in Virgil's Aeneid:

"Monsters more fierce offended Heav'n ne'er sent
From hell's abyss."

"From the mountain-tops, with hideous cry,
And clatt'ring wings, the hungry Harpies fly:
They snatch the meat, defiling all they find.
And, parting, leave a loathsome stench behind."

And of the same extravagant and hideous kidney are chimeras, hydras, ghouls, gorgons, and many another vile product of a twisted imagination which I have neither the space nor the inclination to describe. I must, however, before bringing to a conclusion this division of my subject, fulfill the promise I made to refer to Lilith or the 'night monster' of the Old Testament. In the authorized version of Isaiah xxxiv. 14 there is a passage reading as follows: "The screech owl also shall rest there, and find for herself a place of rest."

In the Revised Version the words 'screech owl' are rendered 'night monster,' with the marginal note Lilith. This is the only place in which 'Lilith' is mentioned, and a very interesting question is raised by the translation of it. According to the Rabbinical idea, Lilith is a specter in the figure of a woman who, entering houses in the dead of night, seizes upon little children and bears them away to murder them. Now, if we turn to the Vulgate version of the Bible, we shall find the above passage rendered: "There hath the lamia lain down and found rest for herself."

SUPERSTITIONS ABOUT ANIMALS

Here we have a similar meaning, the Lilith in this case becoming a lamia or witch. It is quite evident, therefore, that the creature concerned is a 'monster' of evil disposition, and one that is, in popular estimation, to be dreaded. But the passage is far too vague to be able definitely to say what form the 'night monster' takes. In almost every country there is 'a terror by night,' which takes the form of a bird, or beast, or 'bogie,' or something indefinite, but nevertheless horrible and terrifying. Sometimes it is an evil spirit which assumes animal form to perpetrate its villainies. In the East such monsters abound in popular imagination. While in South Africa, I was told about a 'bird of night' whose scream, as it passed over the Boers' houses, made the inhabitants shiver in their beds. In England the 'night-crow' or 'night-raven' formerly created the same terror, though it is more than probable that the monster was nothing worse than some harmless nocturnal bird; at any rate, there is no actual night crow or night-raven in natural history. Several of our poets mention this 'terror by night,' and its associations mark it as an uncanny creature of odious repute:

> "The owl shriek'd at thy birth- an evil sign;
> The night-crow cried, aboding luckless time;
> Dogs howl'd and hideous tempests shook down trees;
> The raven rook'd her on the chimney top."
> -Shakespeare.

> "Here no night-ravenes lodge more black than pitch."
> -Spenser.

> "The shrieks of luckless owls
> We hear, and croaking night-crows in the air."
> -Jonson.

> "Mongst horrid shapes, and shrieks, and sights unholy!
> Find out some uncouth cell,

SUPERSTITIONS ABOUT ANIMALS

Where brooding darkness spreads his jealous wings,
And the night-raven sings."
-Milton.

With these quotations we must leave the subject.
Whether the prophet intended to represent a night monster or a
screech owl is not of very great moment, for either fits
adequately into the scene of desolation which he so strongly
depicts. It will be seen clearly, I hope, from the examples I have
given in this last division of my subject, how busy in the past has
been man's imagination in filling the earth with strange and
mysterious creatures. To endeavor to trace to their fountain-head
the forces which have been at work in the creation of these
monsters, and in forming the superstitions which I have
mentioned in the previous chapters, would be futile- fear,
wonder, reverence, aspiration, all these influences have had a
place. But the days of creation are at an end. If I may put it so,
we are resting now on 'the laurels of the past.' Men in the days
that are gone have done wondrous things with their imagination,
and we of a more prosaic, because perhaps more learned age,
cease to create for ourselves, and look upon the imaginings of
our forefathers with wondering interest.

But much of the superstition we have 'become heirs to' is
likely to die a hard death. Education has done much, but, as I
said at the outset of my writing, education is not of itself a power
which will altogether eradicate superstition. Those who can lay
claim to a wide knowledge of general subjects are not
infrequently superstitious at heart. Nothing but a personal
interest and knowledge of the wonders which abound in natural
history will wipe out the errors. What an entrancing subject lies
at our hands waiting for our investigation! There is no subject
under heaven which will give more pleasure or lasting and real
profit than that of Natural History. The world, with its marvelous
animal life, can have no real beauty or significance for the man

who has never gone deeper than the mere outward, humdrum affairs of life, who has never examined the manifold wonders which abound in the Divine Creation. It requires no imagination, no superstition, to make this Creation glorious! Let us take the simplest flower in the hedgerow, or the frailest insect in the grass, or the tenderest shell in the depths of the ocean, and meditating thereon, we shall stand silent and awed in the presence of Eternal Wisdom.

THE END

www.ingramcontent.com/pod-product-compliance
Lightning Source LLC
Chambersburg PA
CBHW061344250726
48657CB00004B/1319